TENNIS EVERYONE

Fourth Edition

Clancy Moore
and
M.B. Chafin

University of Florida
Gainesville, Florida

 Hunter Textbooks Inc.

Special Acknowledgments:

Cover photo: Copyright 1989 by Tyler Cox. All rights reserved.

Model for cover: Rick Hodge

The Rules of Tennis appearing in the Appendix were provided by the United States Tennis Association and are reprinted with permission.

The photo of the Newport Casino and the historical photos appearing in Chapter 1 were made available through the assistance of the International Tennis Hall of Fame and Tennis Museum, Newport, Rhode Island.

 **Hunter Textbooks Inc.**

823 Reynolda Road
Winston-Salem, North Carolina 27104

Contents

Acknowledgments

The authors would like to express deep appreciation to several individuals who assisted in the preparation of this book. Sincere thanks are in order to Mike Chafin, Doug DeMichele, Coach Steve Breeland and Izel Rivera for the many hours spent on the courts as subjects for photographs; to Al Ring, A.P. Brown, Wayne Sandefur and John Baxter for posing for the doubles photo; and to Dave Smith, Melissa Floyd and P.A. Lee for participating in photographs. The authors are also grateful to Mike Floyd, owner of Court Side Sports, for allowing the use of his well-equipped tennis shop.

A TENNIS MATCH OF YESTERYEAR

Tennis — Today and Yesterday

WHY TENNIS?

At this point you are probably asking yourself, "Why did I choose tennis?" Or perhaps you are already a "sometimes" player and are asking the question, "Why do I continue to play this crazy, frustrating game?"

Whatever your reason, it is possible that in the next few weeks you will arrive at a decision which will affect your lifestyle and habits for the remainder of your life. However, if by chance you should decide that the game of tennis is not for you, at least the decision will be made on the basis of sound information and a fair trial.

As a non-contact support, tennis offers a wide range of diverse benefits to all participants. First and foremost, the game is one of motor skill requiring a strong emphasis on hand-eye coordination with a corresponding emphasis on speed, strength, endurance, and agility. This in no way minimizes the fact that the ability to stroke a tennis ball correctly is fundamental to long-range success. Of equal importance is a mental aspect to the game that is not found in many other athletic endeavors. It is impossible to be a winning tennis player and not be reasonably intelligent. Additionally, you must possess the ability to calculate while engaged in a fiercely contested point. It has been said that perhaps tennis requires more mental involvement from its participants than any other sport.

While many tennis matches have been decided on the durability of their performers, one of the best aspects of the game is that it can be adapted to the participant's age, sex, and level of competition. Like checkers players, older participants frequently develop a seasoned degree of "gamesmanship" which offers some compensation for legs that may have lost their spring. Then there is always the doubles game, which can be enjoyed as long as a person can maintain some degree of mobility. Tennis, as some other sports, also has its own handicapping system. Should you feel you are too accomplished to play with someone, try beginning each game with a one- or two-point deficit and see how quickly the competition is evened!

In terms of a fitness activity, tennis is decidedly better for you than most other sports. Discounting running and swimming, which burn more calories but are boring and repetitious, tennis probably offers more advantages than any other activity. Approximately 40 million people in the United States alone have decided that the idea of burning up to 500 calories an hour, increasing muscle strength without a great increase in muscle size, releasing tension in a wholesome manner, and socializing both for business and pleasure are definitely to their liking. To top it all off, most agree tennis is fun; therefore, it is their answer to the current fitness drive.

Another aspect of tennis which has remained through the years is the capacity for developing true sportsmanship despite the intense competitive nature of the game. The cheating tennis player is an oddity rather than the rule, and whenever players do not conform to the unwritten code, they are quickly abandoned by other players.

In addition, tennis is found and played throughout the world, and the nature of the game is such that both sexes can compete with and against each other.

By this time, you may be convinced that tennis is the game for you and you are anxious to get on the courts. However, there are several points which must be stated so as not to create false illusions.

First of all, tennis need not cost you a lot of money. If you choose to join a private club, play at night or indoors, and purchase the most expensive equipment, the cost could amount to a considerable sum of money. However, if you play on public courts and select moderately priced equipment, the game will cost considerably less than golf, skiing, or boating.

There is another word of caution, and that concerns the mastery of the game. Tennis does require a commitment of time if you really want to improve your level of skill. Unfortunately, it is not one of the easiest games to master. However, almost everyone who perseveres can become reasonably adept at stroking the ball. They may not look and play like professionals but they will derive many of the same benefits which keep most tennis players returning to the courts year after year. Another caution: Once "hooked" you will probably play the game for the rest of your life!

Tennis dress of yesteryear

ORIGIN OF THE GAME

The history of ancient civilizations indicates that a form of tennis was probably played by the early Greeks and Romans. Other evidence indicates that the Chinese were batting a ball back and forth more than 7,000 years ago, and that the Egyptians and Persians also played some kind of a ball and racket game as early a 500 B.C.

The most solid and recent evidence, however, indicates a tennis-like game being played in France about 1200 A.D. The French game called "jeu de paume," or "game of the hand," consisted of hitting a stuffed object over a rope with the bare hand. Rackets did not make an appearance until about 1400 A.D. England and Holland had both accepted the sport by this time and Chaucer referred to the game by using the present name, which is probably a derivative of the French word "tenez."

The game prospered greatly in France and England. However, the French Revolution almost obliterated the sport, since at that time it was considered a game of the rich.

This earliest contest did not much resemble our present game. It was not until 1873 that a British army major by the name of Walter C. Wingfield introduced a new outdoor game which, while incorporating many other aspects, was more similar to our present grass court game. He chose to name his game "Sphairistike," a Greek word meaning "to play." Since the name was too difficult to pronounce, let alone spell, the English quickly began calling the game "tennis on the lawn" and eventually lawn tennis.

The game quickly spread throughout the British empire, and in the year 1874 Mary Outerbridge, who was vacationing in Bermuda, brought the game with her to New York. As a member of Staten Island Cricket Club, she quickly received permission to lay out a court on an unused portion of the cricket grounds.

Although the game was not an overnight success in America, it was only a few years before every major club in the East had courts. Since there was little standardization in these early years, with each club having its own rules, conflicts gradually arose. Finally in 1881, an older brother of Mary Outerbridge convened a meeting of the leading New York clubs to bring some order to the then existing confusion. The outcome of this meeting was the establishment of the United States Lawn Tennis Association, which later became the United States Tennis Association.

The first United States championship was held in Newport, Rhode Island, that same year and was won by Richard Sears, who subsequently defended and held his title for the next six years. In 1915, the tournament was permanently moved to the West Side Tennis Club in Forest Hills, Long Island, and was held there through 1977. In 1978 the tournament was moved to Flushing Meadows, New York.

At approximately the same time, another tournament of tremendous importance was being inaugurated at Wimbledon, England. The subsequent elegance and tradition have established this tournament as perhaps the most important tournament in the world.

A few years later in 1884, Wimbledon began its annual tournament for women, and as the ladies gradually began to shed their voluminous clothing, their game became indistinguishable from that of the men.

The Davis Cup, prestigious award in team tennis

Boris Becker of West Germany made tennis history in July, 1985, when, at the age of 17, he defeated Kevin Curren in the finals of the men's singles at the prestigious Wimbledon Championships. This feat made Becker the youngest player ever to win at Wimbledon. He became an instant hero to the tennis world, primarily due to his youth and his excellent court demeanor.

The Davis Cup, one of the most prestigious awards in tennis, was originated by Dwight Davis who, while still a student at Harvard, donated a cup to be awarded to the winner of a team match between England and the United States. Today this competition has grown to include teams from all over the world and has contributed greatly to world understanding among tennis players.

6

The International Tennis Hall of Fame in Newport, Rhode Island

INTERNATIONAL TENNIS HALL OF FAME

The Newport Casino was the major site of early tennis in the United States. It is the home of the International Tennis Hall of Fame, which houses a modern pro shop, a shop for tennis memorabilia, and a museum of tennis from its early beginnings. Located at the casino is the only "court tennis" court in the United States.

THE GRAND SLAM

The world of tennis recognizes this magnificent achievement as the pinnacle of success. It is very rarely accomplished, and has been achieved by very few players. To win the Grand Slam, a player must win in the same season the championships of Australia, France, England and the United States. While several players, including

Bjorn Borg, have come close, only five have been successful. Two were men and three were women. One player did it twice.

Date	Player
1938	Don Budge (American)
1943	Maureen Connolly (American)
1962	Rod Laver (Australian)
1969	Rod Laver (Australian)
1970	Margaret Court (Australian)
1988	Steffi Graf (West German)

Other tournaments of major importance are:

The Wightman Cup — Annual competition in singles and doubles between women's teams from Great Britain and the United States. It began in 1923.

The Federation Cup — This annual event denotes worldwide competition between women's teams, similar to the Davis Cup. It began in 1963, and has been dominated by Australia and the United States.

CHAPTER 1 EVALUATION

1. What are the motor skills necessary to participate actively in tennis? Explain the importance of each with specific reference to tennis.

2. Why is tennis so popular as an all-round sport to cause 40 million participants to seek opportunities for play annually?

3. The average tennis player can expend how many calories per hour in competition?

4. From a historical viewpoint, tennis can be traced back to the cultures of two areas of civilization. Who were they?

5. The oldest evidence of a racket and ball type game is from which country?

6. Our game of tennis has its positive development in France about 1200 A.D. What was it called in those days?

7. What did the word "Sphairistike" mean and who developed it? Who named our game "lawn tennis"?

8. Tennis was brought to the U.S. by a woman who learned the game in Bermuda. The year was 1874. What was her name?

9. The U.S.L.T.A. first began in the year _____ .
   What does U.S.L.T.A. stand for? _____
   It has changed to the _____
   which stands for _____.

10. The first U.S. Championship was held in 1881 and was won by

_____.

11. What are the three locations of the United States championships to date?

12. What is the most important championship tennis tournament in
the world? Where is it held?

13. International competition for men representing their respective
countries is the _____

14. Name the players who have won the Grand Slam of Tennis.

Name the countries involved in the Grand Slam.

15. What is the difference between the Federation Cup and the
Wightman Cup?

Equipment and Facilities

RACKETS

How much should I spend on a tennis racket? One thing is certain. It is *not* necessary for a beginner to buy a name brand product and spend more than $50-$75 for a racket. As you improve your game, begin to observe other players' rackets and occasionally ask to hit a few balls with various models. This is the only way to determine the true "feel" of a racket and what seems best for you. Many pro shops and dealers now offer prospective customers the opportunity of hitting with different types of rackets.

Does the oversized racket have a greater effective hitting area than the midsize or conventional? Yes, indeed! As you can see in the accompanying illustration, the oversized racket has a much larger effective impact area than smaller rackets.

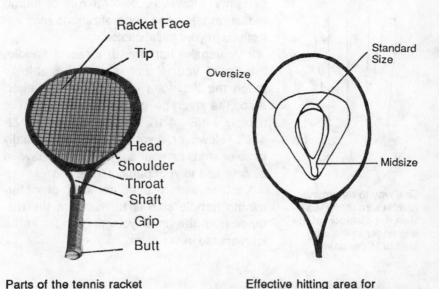

Parts of the tennis racket

Effective hitting area for different racket head sizes

11

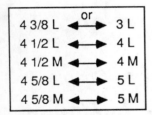

4 3/8 L	or ←→	3 L
4 1/2 L	←→	4 L
4 1/2 M	←→	4 M
4 5/8 L	←→	5 L
4 5/8 M	←→	5 M

Markings on Racket Handle

One way to determine handle size is to measure the distance of the ring finger to the long crease in the palm.

What do the various markings on the handle of my racket mean? If you have markings, you probably have a quality racket. The numbers and letters themselves indicate the handle size, weight of the frame, and sometimes special model numbers. Handle sizes are indicated by the numbers 4 3/8, 4 1/2, 4 5/8 and 4 3/4. Some recent models use only the numbers 3, 4, 5, and 6 to designate 3/8, 4/8, 5/8, and 6/8. See the accompanying chart.

Racket weight is usually designated by the letters L, M, or H immediately following the handle size. The letters indicate a range in ounces and may vary according to manufacturer; however, L (light) rackets usually weigh less than 13-14 ounces. H (heavy) rackets will weigh more than 14 ounces, and M (medium) rackets will range somewhere in between the two.

But what about me—what size and weight should I have? At this point in your tennis career, it is impossible to say with certainty. However, several rule-of-thumb measurements and generalizations may assist you in your initial choice.

If you shake hands with a racket handle, the tip of your thumb should be able to touch the first joint of your middle finger. Also, the average grip size for women is usually 4 3/8 - 4 1/2 and for men it is 4 1/2 - 4 5/8. However, if your hands are unusually large or small for your sex, this would have to be adjusted to your particular case.

Another widely used method of determining handle size is to measure the distance from the tip of your ring finger to the long crease in the palm.

Selecting the proper racket is an important part of the game.

If your present grip is too large, your arm will probably be tiring very quickly. If the grip is too small, the racket will twist more readily in your hand, making it appear that you are not gripping the handle tightly enough.

Several friends have been telling me that I need a lighter racket, but I don't really know whether I do or not. Can you help me? Probably not, since your size or strength makes a difference. However, certain facts may help you make a good decision.

1. Experts generally agree that rackets weighing under 11.5 ounces are too light; conversely, rackets over 14 ounces are probably too heavy.

2. Research indicates that for swings of equal speed, the medium-weight racket hits the ball deeper and faster than the light racket. This assumes the rackets are identical except for weight. So it seems the best advice is to *pick the heaviest racket that you can handle comfortably.*

Baseliners generally use a head-heavy frame while serve-and-volley players usually prefer a head-light frame. To determine your racket's status, adjust it on a thin balance point until it is perfectly balanced, mark the point, then measure from that point to the tip of the head. If the racket is 27 inches long, the balance point should be 13 1/2 inches. If the balance point is closer to the head, it is head-heavy, and if it is closer to the handle, the racket is head-light.

I have heard a lot about flex or flexibility in rackets. Is this important? In general, wooden rackets are stiffer than metal rackets, but there is a wide range of differences within each category. Metal, or very flexible rackets, tend to provide more power but less control. A stiffer frame will give a player less power but more control. From a beginner's standpoint, *control* is far more important than speed.

How strong and how stiff are graphite and boron compared to wood? Graphite is about 20 times stiffer and stronger, and boron is even more.

How did we get into all of these exotic materials used in racket making? Until the late 1960s, almost all rackets were made of wood. From a plus standpoint, the wood racket was cheap, absorbed vibrations, and had good feel. Its weakness was wearability; i.e., it abraded easily and weakened with use.

About 1970 Wilson had broken through with its highly-touted T-2000 and the marketing race was on. However, it was the creation of the oversized racket in the mid-1970s that forced the development of lighter and stronger materials necessary for the increased size rackets.

Remember that all rackets, even the most expensive, tend to deteriorate with time. This results in loss of power and control; however, the harder substances lose their strength and stiffness more slowly.

Why do some of the more expensive rackets such as graphite and boron get such poor marks for abrasion resistance? Many of these so-called miracle fibers wear very quickly. Also, because of their hardness, they tend to be brittle and chip when striking the court surface. Because of this, some manufacturers feature a hard strip of nylon or polyurethane around the outer frame of the racket. Others have developed a replaceable bumper guard for protection. A simple and inexpensive protection in use for years on wooden rackets is hospital tape or rubberized electrical tape.

Could you give me some idea of the relative cost, strength, stiffness, etc., of the various racket materials? The accompanying racket materials chart may help. Note that the ratings range from 1-8, with 1 being the most or best.

RACKET MATERIALS CHART*

Material	Cost	Strength	Abrasion Resistant	Stiffness	Vibration Absorption
Wood	Least Expensive (1)	8	8	8	1
Boron	Most Expensive (8)	2	7	1	5
Steel	Cheap (2)	6	1	2	6
Aluminum	Cheap (3)	7	1	6	6
Titanium	Moderate (4)	5	1	4	6
Fiberglass	Moderate (4)	4	4	7	2
Kevlar	Expensive (5)	3	5	5	3
Graphite	Expensive (6)	1	6	3	4

*Rackets range from 1-8 with one being the most or best according to category.

I have great difficulty in controlling the additional power generated by the mid- and oversized racket. Any advice? If you have a wristy, floppy, short swing, you are in trouble. To be effective with an oversized racket, try swinging in a smooth, fluid manner and go for a stiffer racket rating. A relatively stiff swing with little wrist usually works best.

What size handles do the pros use? Sixteen quarterfinalists in a recent tournament were surveyed with the following results: of eight men, two used 4 1/2 and six used 4 5/8; of eight women, two used 4 3/8, four used 4 1/2 and two used 4 5/8.

What about string pressure for this same group? Of eight men, three used 61 pounds or less, three used 62-64 pounds, one used 66-68 pounds and one used 80-90 pounds; of eight women, two used 57-58 pounds, four used 59-63 pounds, and two used 70-74 pounds.

Examples of modern rackets

Is there a racket larger than the Prince® and is it legal?
We now have the Weed ® racket and, yes, it is larger than the
Prince® and it is legal. As a matter of fact, the Weed® has 135
square inches of face. This makes it twice as large as the old
conventional racket and 25% larger than the Prince®. Despite a net
advantage most tournament players have shied away from it so far.

**A friend has offered me a "used" racket. How can I tell
if it is a "quality" racket?** The first thing to do is to examine the
frame for warping and cracks or, if a metal frame, look for flex cracking
and dents. Wooden rackets tend to crack first in the extreme bottom
and top positions of the racket head. The handle positions should
be of good quality leather and not have staples or nails exposed to
the sight. The head of the racket should contain seven to twelve
laminations as do more expensive rackets. If the racket is metal, are
the welding and riveting secure? The general workmanship and
finish will also provide some indication of quality. Also, do not forget
that many of the better rackets have permanent markings on the side
of the racket indicating size and weight.

How many times can my racket be restrung? This depends upon the initial quality of your racket and how you take care of it. A reasonable expectation would be four to six times over a period of two or three years.

What are some of the more important aspects of modern-day rackets?

Vibration Damping Rating: Indicates how quickly impact vibrations disappear.

Power Zone Rating: This zone is usually located just below the sweet spot center. Balls striking above the power zone tend to lose power as they move nearer the top of the racket.

Sweet Spot: The point on the racket face giving the least vibrations on ball contact.

Overall Stiffness Rating: Indicates "racket feel" to a player. One to four is usually very flexible. Six to ten usually denotes a stiff racket. Stiff rackets typically provide more power and consistency.

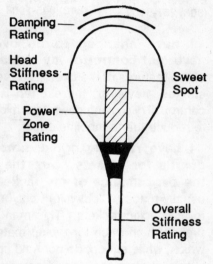

What are the latest trends in rackets? There are so many ongoing innovations and experiments that the answer is tough. The one thing you will see more and more of is the "wide body" frame. This will make rackets stiffer and should increase the power potential of a racket.

Grips— More synthetics and less leather.

Head size—At one time a 110-square-inch racket was considered to be an oversized racket, and an 85-square-inch racket was classified as mid-sized. Now the sizes seem to be averaging 95-105 square inches.

Racket Weight— Racket weights continue to become lighter and are now down to around 12 1/3 ounces. Racket heads are also lighter; extra head weight can be added using lead tape.

I am interested in contacting racket companies for their literature. Can you help me? Most pro shops will carry some literature; however, here are the addresses for five popular companies:

DONNAY
P.O. Box 910
Williston, VT 05495
(800) 258-8291

HEAD
4801 North 63rd St.
Boulder, CO 80301
(800) 257-5100

PRINCE
P.O. Box 2031
Princeton, NJ 08543-2031
(800) 2 TENNIS

PRO-KENNEX
9606 Kearney Villa Rd.
San Diego, CA 92126
(800) 845-1908

YAMAHA
P.O. Box 6600
Buena Park, CA 90620
(714) 522-9011

I have changed to an oversized racket but seem to have lost control of my shots. What do you suggest? One of the features of the oversized racket is increased power on ground strokes; however, there often is an accompanying loss of shot control. Try moving down to a mid-sized racket or string more tightly to reduce the trampoline effect.

I have recently noted more and more bumper or frame guards for rackets. Are they necessary? Can they affect the performance of my racket? Bumper or frame guards are usually made of lightweight polyurethane or nylon and are designed to fit specific rackets. This market has developed because of the present high price for racket materials such as boron and graphite which, while strong, do not hold up well to court contact. Most older tennis players have used some type of tape to achieve the same purpose—it just doesn't look quite as classy.

In terms of equipment, which brands seem to be the most popular among tournament players? The first thing you have to remember is that many high-class tournament players are paid to use certain brands. However, a recent prestigious American tournament indicated the following:

	#1	#2	#3
Rackets	Prince	Wilson	Head
Clothing	Adidas	Nike	
Shoes	Adidas	Nike	Reebok

I have heard that there is a trend toward stiffer rackets. Is this true or not? True. Stiffness appears to be the new "in" thing for tennis rackets. Apparently the more control and better "feel" advocates are winning out. One lab team that tests new tennis rackets reports that 1989's crop was almost one point stiffer than those measured during the prior three years.

What future changes do you see in equipment? That is a tough question since predicting the future is generally "by guess and by golly." However, the mid-sized rackets (85 square inches) will probably increase another 10 square inches or so; present oversized rackets (110 square inches) may do likewise; strings will become thinner, will wear longer, and will be strung less tightly.

Can the choice of tennis balls make a difference in winning or losing? Yes, indeed! The authors once had a tennis opponent who always wanted to use heavy duty tennis balls. Of course, he was a baseline player and hit the ball less forcefully than most of his opponents. Heavy duty balls tend to fuzz up more and this slows play. If you prefer a serve-and-volley game, then insist on the lighter felt balls.

I recently had my racket restrung at high tension and played very well for a while. Then as the strings lost tension I seemed to lose control of my shots. Is there a way to check string tension so that I might know when to restring or switch to another racket? The professionals usually gauge this by feel and sound; however, since most of us are not able to play every day, we fail to develop this ability. Currently on the market are two devices that measure string tension in a racket. The Stringmeter MK-VI® sells for about $15-20, and the less portable (but more accurate) Flex II® price tag is approximately $120. The Stringmeter is a small plastic device that fits into any tennis cover or bag. The Flex II involves a metal racket support, a sophisticated pressure gauge, and is much more bulky.

I have a terrible time trying to store that second tennis ball. Any suggestions? Most tennis clothing for men has side pockets; however, many female tennis panties are not so equipped, hence the question. One make of panties, called Poc-a-Ball,® is reasonably priced and is found at most tennis shops. Another product from West Germany is called Ballclip.® The plastic ballholder clips onto the waistband. Either of these might help.

I have a problem with smelly feet which, of course, influences my tennis shoes. Even though I bathe regularly, people walk away from me. What can I do? This is an interesting phenomenon which affects many people. Try one of the odor-prevention products available in the foot-care section of the drugstore. They are inexpensive and may be trimmed down with scissors to fit any shoe.

Assuming use of the same material, is there any difference in using a 3/4" grip wrapping as opposed to 1"? Because the 3/4" grip is narrower, there will be more turns around the handle and less distance between the grooves. Some players believe that more depressions or grooves on the handle give better racket control through reduced slippage. The 1" grip with fewer grooves does seem to be more comfortable.

What are the advantages of synthetic grips as opposed to leather? It is generally agreed that moisture is the chief cause of racket slippage. Leather tends to be brittle and lacks moisture absorbent qualities at around 50°. At 90° it absorbs well but quickly becomes saturated.

On the other hand, synthetic wrapping can absorb moisture up to 9 or 10 times better and will give up internal moisture if wiped with a towel. Therefore, many players feel a synthetic grip will provide a more secure grip in high humid temperatures.

My racket grip gets very sweaty, dirty, and slick during summer play. Is there any way to clean it? Most professionals agree that the racket grip must be clean and slightly tacky for expert performance. For best results, obtain a stiff bristle brush, water, and biodegradable soap. Wet the grip, soap it down and scrub thoroughly. Then rinse and allow to dry. As a final step, rebrush the dry grip to restore its tack.

What are the racket differences between the pros and the average public? There are some commonalities which can be used by all players. First of all, the pros know that very stiff rackets can be hard on the arm and shoulder; also, a medium flex racket provides better touch and feel. In terms of weight, most play with the heaviest racket they can handle according to their game, i.e., baseline or serve volley. Most tend to have frame heads light in balance while the heavy groundstrokers generally have a heavier weighted head.

In terms of racket string, pros tend to prefer thin, gut string. The advantage is increased liveness and a better bite on the ball. The disadvantages are lack of durability and cost.

STRINGS

Racket strings have a self-contained vocabulary. The more important terms are as follows:

Gauge: This represents the diameter of a string. The thinner the string, the higher the number. Thus an 18 gauge string would be thinner than a 15 or 16 gauge. Generally, the thicker the string the more durable, and the thinner the string the more responsive.

Tensile Strength: This is a measure of overall strength. Synthetic strings range from about 140 pounds to over 220 pounds.

Elongation: This represents the amount of potential stretch in a string. All strings have some stretch, but excessive elongation will produce a sawing action and more wear, plus a lowering in tension. Strings range from about 5% (gut) to 18% (monofiliment nylon) with the majority averaging around 10%.

Almost all strings may be classified into one of the following groups:

Monofilament Nylon — This string evolved in the 1950s as the first synthetic racket string. It is a relatively weak string, utilizing one strand of thick nylon, which is highly susceptible to temperature variances and elongation.

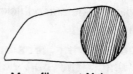

Monofilament Nylon

Core String — This is a highly durable string and is the most commonly found. It consists of a single or multiple core surrounded by individual nylon fibers. A core string is usually coated with urethane for protection against moisture.

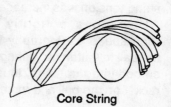

Core String

Twisted Fibers String — This string is made by twisting multiple nylon fibers and bonding them together with urethane. A urethane outer coating is also applied for added protection.

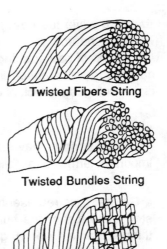

Twisted Fibers String

Twisted Bundles String

Natural Gut

Twisted Bundles String — This is a modification of the twisted fibers string where several bundles of twisted fibers are themselves twisted and encased in a urethane coating.

Natural Gut String — Natural strips of sheep or cow intestines are twisted and bonded together. The string plays well but is vulnerable to water and wear. Less than 5% of all rackets are now strung with gut.

How did the term "synthetic gut" originate? String manufactures have long sought a substitute for regular gut. They found that the best gut string used about 15 strands of intestinal fibers twisted together. Thus, because the early strings were made of synthetic nylon fibers twisted together, the term "synthetic gut" was applied. Some types of "synthetic gut" strings are: Prime synthetic, Babolot Trueshot, Babolot Fineplay, Performance Plus, Topspin, Head Hot Shot, Tournament 20 Elite, Limelite, Duralite, and Redline. The string thickness is measured numerically with 15 gauge being average.

Does string tension influence the velocity (i.e., speed) at which the ball comes off the strings? Research has shown that when using gut and nylon, ball velocity decreased when string tension was increased from 50 to 65 pounds.

How does a tightly strung racket affect ball control? High speed photography indicates that high string tension causes the ball to flatten out during impact. This causes the nap of the ball to embed into the string, thus affording a greater "biting action" of the racket on the ball and more control.

Another explanation is that when a racket is strung very tightly the ball is on the face of the racket for a shorter length of time; therefore, because most balls are hit off center, the racket face has more time to rotate on impact thus sending the ball off in errant flight.

How can I increase my ability to impart spin to the balls? One easy way is to string at a lower or middle tension. Less string tension also aids in the case of tennis elbow, since less tension enhances vibration damping.

Why are natural gut strings so expensive? Racket gut usually comes from the external portion of beef intestines because these have the greatest amount of elasticity. And since only two or three strips out of each intestine are considered usable—it costs. It takes about two cows to provide enough gut for one racket.

Should you use the same thickness of string to play on clay or rubico as opposed to a hard surface? Since soft surface play is much slower resulting in longer points and matches and more wear, most tournament players and professionals prefer a string one gauge thicker than when playing on a hard surface. Another factor is moisture, which is frequently associated with soft surfaces, and the increased abrasiveness resulting as both ball and strings pick up gritty particles.

How often should I have my racket restrung? Research has shown that from the day your racket is strung, the strings slowly but surely lose their tension. Most experts feel that if you are a frequent player a good rule of thumb is to restring as many times in a year as you play in a week. Of course, if you are a spin artist, you will likely go through a set of strings at a faster pace. If you are a "sometimes" player most people feel you should restring at least twice yearly.

How can I tell if my stringer has done a good job for me? There are five basic things to look for:

String Burns — If a stringer pulls the cross strings too hard and fast, a grooving or notching effect will result. The notching will come with normal wear and play, but if made during stringing, will cause premature string breakage.

Empty String Holes — String holes are put in rackets for a purpose. They should be filled.

Overlaps or Crossovers — Overlapping string at the top of your racket will expose it to all the wear and tear of normal play. Of course, if you never scrape the top of your racket on low shots, you won't have a problem.

Tubing — Tubing should be used on broken or cracked grommets. Take care that the tubing does not extend more than 1/8 inch above the frame.

Uneven Weave — A missed weave pattern is an example of sloppy work.

I like to put lots of spin on the ball. Any suggestions as to choice of string? There is a great deal of experimentation presently going on in regard to string shape, gauge, and compositions. However, the most important consideration is gauge or thickness. The newest thing seems to be a 16 to 17 gauge "micro" string. It is thought that the thinner string creates wider spaces or openings in grid pattern which allows the ball to sink in farther; thus, increasing the "bite" or opportunity for more spin. Remember also that low string tension produces more power and less control while high string tension provides less power but greater control.

TENNIS BALLS

Basically there are four different kinds of tennis balls: regular, heavy duty, pressureless and high altitude. Heavy duty balls are made for hard abrasive surfaces and have substances such as nylon and dacron in the covering. Regular balls contain more wool in the covering thus making a tighter nap so as to pick up less dirt. Since there is no appreciable pressure within pressureless balls, they are able to last until the ball core loses it resiliency. However, they seem to feel heavy and have a peculiar sound when hit. Thus, they are not popular in the United States. High altitude balls contain less air pressure within the ball so as to equalize the atmospheric conditions of being at a higher elevation.

What kind of tennis balls should I buy? Tennis balls are as varied as automobiles. In this case, it is probably wise to stick to better known name brands. Costs will vary but usually range from $2

When choosing tennis balls, it is best to stay with name brands.

to $4 per can of three. Players who play on firm abrasive surfaces such as rough concrete or asphalt will realize some savings if they purchase only heavy duty balls which have an extra heavy covering of felt. Tennis ball quality is determined by standardized requirements, and manufacturers who meet this standard will display a "USTA Approved" stamp on their merchandise.

Most manufacturers inflate their balls with compressed air or gas and pack them in pressurized containers. As you open a new can you should hear a pronounced hissing sound which indicates that the pressure has been maintained. Once opened, balls rapidly lose their resiliency. Should you open a can and not hear this sound, simply return your purchase and most retailers will gladly exchange the can for you. Also, any ball that cracks or breaks early in play should be returned for replacement. One way to check a set of opened balls quickly is to squeeze them for firmness and to drop for bounce. Any ball that appears unusually soft or does not bounce at least knee high has probably lost its compression. Heavily worn balls tend to become unduly light, and some balls that become shaggy in wear tend to collect moisture during play, thus becoming very "heavy" and slow. Even new, unopened tennis balls that have been stored for several months tend to lose some of their vitality.

How are tennis balls made? Tennis balls are two half-spheres of rubber bonded together and covered with glued fabric. These hourglass-shaped pieces of fabric contain combinations of nylon, dacron, wool and cotton depending upon the specifications of a particular manufacturer.

How are tennis balls pressurized? Balls made in the United States are pressurized by placing the two halves inside a heated pressure chamber. They are then bonded together and when removed, the ball has acquired the pressure of the chamber. Other manufacturers achieve pressurization by inserting small amounts of water and a vaporized chemical into the halves. Then the rubber core is sealed and heated causing the chemical to pressurize the interior of the ball. The approximate interval pressure is 11-14 pounds per square inch.

What about balls that are advertised as pressureless? These balls have a thicker and more "bouncy" core than pressurized balls. While they have a heavier feel and do not bounce quite as high, they are less influenced by climate and last longer than regular pressurized balls.

Are yellow balls better than white? With the advent of more artificial lighting, "optic" yellow balls came into vogue. They are also more visible against a bright sky in outdoor play. White balls are now very scarce.

How long can tennis balls be kept in a sealed can? Recent technology has drastically reduced the number of cans that lose their pressure even though they have an unbroken seal. The average shelf life of a sealed can of pressurized balls now approximates 1-2 years.

Should I buy regular or extra heavy tennis balls? The type of tennis balls you choose depends upon the court surface you play on. The basic difference is the nap, or cover. Heavy duty balls fluff up more quickly and this helps to protect the cover against abrasive wear. Regular balls have a tighter nap so as to not pick up as much grit or particles. Heavily fluffed balls also tend to pick up moisture quickly thus making them heavier and, in effect, slowing the pace of a game.

TENNIS SHOES

I have heard a lot of talk about types or kinds of feet. How can I determine what type of foot I have? There are basically three types of feet. They are "normal" foot, the "hyper-mobile flat foot," and the "high arch cavus foot." To determine your type, start by getting an imprint to determine how how your feet react to your body weight.

There are two ways to do this. One is to simply wet your feet and stand on an absorbent flat surface. Another way is to trace your feet on paper. Either way, they should be traced while sitting down, while standing on both feet, and then when standing on one foot. Now compare your drawing to the drawing below.

If you have a normal foot the arch will collapse only a little when standing on both feet. This type of foot absorbs shock reasonably well and should cause few problems if running under 20 miles per week. The normal foot needs a moderately stiff shoe having a moderate amount of shock absorbency.

The hypermobile flat foot appears to be normal with no weight on it. However, when full weight is placed on both feet, the arch collapses. When all the weight is placed on one foot, the arch almost disappears. This type of foot requires a shoe which provides motion control and firm support.

The high arch cavus foot tracing will change very little from a sitting to standing position. Even with all your weight on one foot there will be very little change in the tracing. This kind of foot is fairly rigid, has

Hypermobile
Flat Foot

Normal Foot

High Arch
Cavus Foot

THREE TYPES OF FEET

less motion, and absorbs shock poorly. If you have this type of foot you need a shoe that is more flexible, softer, and has more cushioning to absorb shock.

What does the word "lasting" mean? "Lasting" is very important to shoe construction in terms of flexibility and curvature of the shoe. "Board lasting" gives less shock absorption, but provides a very stiff, stable shoe. "Slip lasting," on the other hand, is more shock absorbing, less stiff, and less stable. Proper lasting depends on several things, including type of foot, type of running, body weight, and running surface.

What about polyurethane soled shoes? Are they better than rubber shoes? Urethane shoes are generally lighter than rubber and, in some cases, may wear longer than rubber. However, there seems to be a direct correlation between slipperiness and durability; i.e., the more durable the more slippery, particularly in late night or early morning play where moisture may be a factor.

There are so many different patterns and tread designs on the soles of tennis shoes. Which is the best? Many years ago, sailing enthusiasts developed a herringbone pattern for shoes used on slippery decks. This "deck sole" is still superior for almost any surface. It does have the disadvantage of sometimes collecting sand or particles in the fine treads which are later deposited in the car or home.

I have exceptionally weak ankles. Is there any particular shoe that is better than the others? Here are some suggestions:

— Rehabilitate your ankle with specific exercises following every injury.

— There are 3/4 cut shoes (in between a basketball shoe and the low cut oxford) that offer greater protection than the usual tennis shoe.

— Be wary of super-cushioned shoes. They cause your foot to sit higher in the shoe, thus the foot is less stable. A more rigid heel counter also helps support and stabilize the ankle.

Must I buy special clothing to play tennis? This depends upon where you choose to play and how important conformity is to you. Tennis players have probably been brainwashed more than any other sports person as to proper attire. It is true that many private clubs have strict written and unwritten rules governing the dress of court participants. Certainly, whether you wear a pair of basketball or track shorts rather than tennis shorts is not going to influence the quality of your game unless you feel self-conscious. What is important is that you wear light-colored clothing and a head covering if playing in intense heat. Also, whatever you choose to wear should be comfortable to you. Many synthetics, while holding an excellent press, do not have absorbent qualities, thus causing great discomfort to wearers. Cotton remains one of the best fabrics for tennis attire.

Proper tennis attire depends on where you play and how fashion-conscious you are.

Tennis shoes may be one exception. Certainly if you play on any soft surface, such as clay or rubico, you must have relatively smooth-soled sneakers and no heels. Basketball or jogging shoes are not suitable since their soles are too deeply indented and leave court marks. If you are to enjoy the game, it is a necessity that your feet be reasonably well cared for. This means that if you play on a very hard surface you should have cushioned insoles for better comfort. Leather-topped shoes offer a little additional support but tend to cause more sweating since they do not have "breathing" ability. They are also more expensive.

Tennis socks are equally important since they can easily affect the condition of your feet. For the most comfort, they should be a mixture of cotton and wool and have great absorbent qualities. Many tennis players always wear two pairs of socks to facilitate this.

Warm-up suits or jackets are necessary for comfort if you move from a hot court to indoor air-conditioning or if you choose to play on cold windy days.

Wristlets and sweat bands are very convenient and necessary if you play a vigorous game in hot humid climates.

Light colored cotton clothing is the best choice of apparel for the tennis court.

As a tennis player, you can choose clothes that are fashionable, proper, comfortable, or all three!

TENNIS COURTS

While tennis court dimensions are standardized by the governing agencies of tennis, court composition and court settings are as varied as tennis players themselves. In general, types of courts will be determined by climate and area of the country. Most good courts do have some standardized features, however. First of all, they will be laid out on a north-south line to minimize sun problems, and they will usually be fenced and surrounded by large hedges and/or green plastic saran windbreaker to further decrease the effects of wind and to increase ball visibility.

Tennis courts are laid out on a north-south line and are usually surrounded by hedges or fencing, with windbreakers.

32

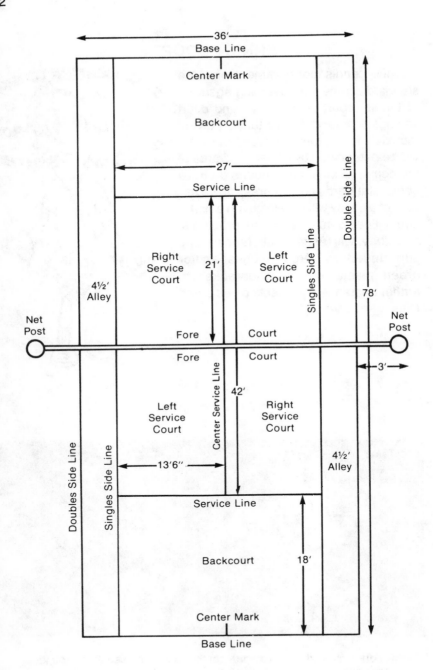

Standard Dimensions of a Tennis Court

Soft Courts

The South probably has a higher proportion of soft courts than any other area of the United States. The most common materials are clay, rubico, and Har-tru®. Soft courts have the advantage of being easy on the feet and legs. In addition, the style of play is slower, the ball tends to "sit up" more and the speed will be taken off the "big hitter." Soft courts tend to favor a soft hitter and to diminish the attacking player's game.

The primary disadvantage of soft surfaces is the difficulty of keeping them in good playing condition. They must be swept, watered, and rolled daily. Also, a freezing climate will cause the court lines to pull out of the ground, and should players be allowed to use a recently thawed or very wet court, damage can easily occur which might take weeks to repair. Some porous types, however, do have the advantage of quickly absorbing a hard summer shower and being ready for play in less than an hour.

Measuring for proper height.

Hard Courts

Hard courts of asphalt, wood, composition materials, and cement are more common in the United States than other parts of the world. The Western states have traditionally emphasized this type of court. This surface has a number of advantages, with a minimum amount of upkeep being the most prominent feature. Other assets include a uniform ball bounce and increased visibility.

The primary disadvantage of hard surfaces is the wear and tear induced upon a player's feet, legs and shoes. Of course, the pace of play is generally much faster since the ball rebounds quickly from this type of surface, thus favoring the driving hitter and big server. However, the surface of a hard court can be modified by the contractor to provide slow, medium or fast play.

Nets and Accessories

Tennis nets are generally made of synthetic materials such as nylon or polyethylene to restrict the effects of moisture. Manufacturers employing the use of cotton or natural fibers generally dip their nets in a cresote-tar substance to retard the rotting process. Metal nets, while durable, have a tendency to bow in or out, thus creating inaccuracies in net height and distance from the net to the baseline. Center straps are necessary on all but metal nets since it is very difficult to achieve a fine adjustment with the windlass on the net post.

CHAPTER 2 EVALUATION

1. How does one determine the proper handle size and weight of the racket?

2. What are the various playing qualities of strings and tightness or looseness in stringing?

3. Contrast the advantages and disadvantages of soft courts vs hard courts.

4. Contrast the quality of flexibility in tennis rackets. What are the advantages and disadvantages of racket flex?

5. What qualities should tennis clothes possess?

6. Name the lines and areas of a tennis court.

7. What are the changes that have occurred in the styles and colors of tennis clothing over the history of the game?

8. Name the parts of a tennis racket.

9. What are the differences in nylon and gut strings? Name some advantages and disadvantages.

10. What is the "average" racket grip size? Weight?

11. What are the advantages of polyurethane soled shoes?

12. If you are a "soft hitter" what type of court will favor your game?

Chapter 3

Scoring and Playing the Game

First of all, it helps greatly if you know the rules. However, these are usually written in a technical language and specific points are often hard to find when needed. In addition, a number of "unwritten" rules, while not specifically covered by the rules book, are nonetheless very important to the game and, of course, to you. See the Appendix for the complete Rules of Tennis.

From a teaching standpoint the following questions and points of procedure seem to be the most relevant and are most asked by beginners.

What is a game and how do I keep score?
The points are:

No points or 0 = LOVE
One point = 15
Two points = 30
Three points = 40
Four points = game (if two points ahead of opponent)

UNITS OF SCORING

Points
↓
Games
↓
Sets
↓
Match

If the players' scores are even after six or more points in a game, the score is referred to as deuce. Should the server go ahead by one point after deuce the score becomes Advantage Server or "Ad in," and should the server win the next point, it is "Game." However, if the score is tied after six or more points and the receiver wins the next point after deuce, then the score becomes Advantage Receiver or "Ad out." If the receiver wins the next point it becomes his or her "Game."

What is a set? A set is a part of a match that is completed when a person or team wins at least six games and is ahead by at least two games as 6-1, 6-2, 7-5, 8-6, etc.

What is a tie breaker? The tie breaker is a fairly recent innovation used to complete a set when the game score becomes 6-6. This prevents long, drawn-out contests which may be detrimental to players.

THE 9 POINT TIE BREAKER

Singles: In singles if player A is due to serve the next regular game, A serves two points as in normal play, starting from the right side. Then the serve goes to the other side with player B doing the same. After these four points the players change sides and the service again goes to player A, who serves the next two points. If a winner has not yet been determined the serve again goes to player B, and B serves two points. At this time, should the score be tied four all, player B serves point nine. However, A, who is the receiver, may elect to receive the serve from either the right or left service court. The players do not change courts after the set and player B begins serving the first game of the new set.

Doubles: Here, assume team A-B is playing team C-D: A and C serve the first four points, sides are changed, and B-D serve the next four. Should a ninth point be necessary, player D serves the third serve. Remember, players always must serve from the same side they have been serving from.

THE 12 POINT TIE BREAKER

The 12 point tie breaker has become the most popular tie breaker used today. Normally in the U.S. this tie breaker — or any tie breaker — goes into effect when the set score reaches 6-all, but at the option of the Tournament Committee it may take effect at 8-all in one or more complete rounds. Also, the ITF description indicates that the tie breaker normally would not be used in the third or fifth set of a best of three or best of five match, but any nation has the option of stipulating, in a given tournament, that the tie breaker will be in effect even in those identifiable final sets of matches. Here is the procedure:

Singles: A serves first point from right court; B serves points 2 and 3 (left and right); A serves points 4 and 5 (left and right); B serves point 6 (left) and after they change ends, point 7 (right); A serves points 8 and 9 (left and right); B serves point 10 and 11 (left and right), and A serves point 12 (left). If points reach 6-all, players change ends and continue as before. A serves point 13 (right); B serves points 14 and 15 (left and right); etc., until one player establishes a margin of two points. Players change ends for one game to start the next set, with player B to serve first.

Doubles: Follow the same pattern, with partners preserving the sequence of their serving turns.

Assuming A & B vs C & D: Player A serves first point (right); C serves points 2 and 3 (left and right); B serves points 4 and 5 (left and right); D serves point 6 (left) and after teams change ends, point 7 (right). A serves points 8 and 9 (left and right); C serves points 10 and 11 (left and right), and B serves point 12 (left). If points reach 6-all, teams change ends and continue as before — B serves point 13 (right); D serves points 14 and 15 (left and right); etc., until one team establishes a margin of two points. Teams change ends for one game to start the next set. A tie breaker game counts as one game in reckoning time between ball changes.

VASSS "NO-AD" SCORING

The "No-Ad" procedure is simply and precisely what the name implies: a player need win only four points to win a game. That is, if the score goes to 3-points-all (or deuce) the next point decides the game — it is game point for both players. The receiver has the right to choose to which court the service is to be delivered on the seventh point.

If a "No-Ad" set reaches 6-games-all, a tie breaker shall be used which normally would be the 5-of-9. However, in collegiate tennis, the 12 point tie breaker is used.

NOTE: The score-calling may be either in the conventional terms or in simple numbers; i.e., "zero, one, two, three, game." The latter is usually preferred.

Then who wins the contest or match? Most competitive matches are determined by whoever wins two of the three sets. However, some prestigious matches and tournaments are determined by the best three out of five sets.

Are balls that hit the boundary line good? Yes.

What is a let serve and how many times can a person have a let serve? A let serve occurs when a serve hits the top of the net and falls into the proper service area. There is no limit to the number of let serves a person may have.

Balls that hit boundary lines are good.

What if a point other than a serve hits the top of the net and falls into my opponents court? It is a great shot on your part, and must be returned by your opponent.

If I make a poor toss on the serve, can I catch the ball rather than trying to hit it? Yes, but it is a fault if you swing and miss.

What if my opponent allows the ball from a previous point to remain on his court and I hit the ball during a succeeding rally? It is a great shot on your part and your point if the correct ball is not returned.

Can I throw my racket at the ball and hit it? No.

My doubles partner has a pitty-pat serve and I am getting killed trying to play the net when he serves. What should I do? Our first advice would be to get a new partner. However, since this may not be practical, we suggest backing up to the baseline, at least on all second serves.

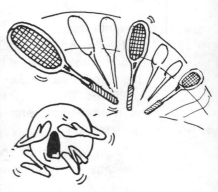

My partner does not see very well and returns serves that are frequently faults. Is it legal for me to call serves directed to him, out? Yes, it is your responsibility.

It is not legal to throw your racket at the ball.

In doubles, can the best serving partner serve first at the beginning of each set? Yes, this is generally a good idea unless the sun or wind causes unusual problems for your partner.

What is a pro-set? A pro-set is one in which a person or team wins at least eight games and is ahead by at least two games. Example: 8-0; 8-1; 8-2 etc.

What keeps the score? One of the nice things about tennis is that players usually keep their own score. Other than some tournaments in which the umpire will call out the score, it is usually the server's responsibility to call out the score.

Can a player touch the net or reach over the net to hit the ball? A player may not touch the net while play is in progress and may not reach over the net unless the ball has first bounced on his side and then been carried back across by the wind or severe backspin.

Who serves first in a match? It is customary to flip a coin or spin the racket. The winner has the choice of serving, receiving, or choice of court. The loser has the remaining choice.

What if a ball rolls across my court when a point is being played? A let or replay is in order if it immediately called for. Do not wait until you see if you win or lose the point before calling "Let."

Can I serve the ball underhanded? Yes.

Can I have some rest in a two out of three set match? Technically no, in men's competition. However, in informal

---

Learn to Score

— Conventional Scoring
— Vasss No-Ad
— Pro Sets
— 9 pt. Tie Breaker
— 12 pt. Tie Breaker

Can we flip for serve?

play it is fairly common. In female competition there may be a 10-minute rest period between the second and third set.

What is a foot fault? A foot fault occurs whenever the server makes contact on or within the baseline before hitting the ball. The offending player loses that opportunity to put the ball in play.

Do players ever change ends of the court? Yes, at the completion of games 1, 3, 5, 7, 9, etc., in each set, and in the case of tie breakers.

What happens if I allow a ball to hit me or I catch it while I am outside of the court? This is technically illegal and must be considered a good shot for your opponent even though it is obviously an out shot. Always let the ball go to prevent hassles.

Can I yell or deliberately distract my opponent like I do in basketball and football? No.

What if I blinked just as my opponent's shot hit the court and I was not sure whether it was in or out? Always give your opponent the benefit of the doubt. Do not play the ball and then call it out. Remember that each player is responsible for calling out balls on his or her side of the court.

What if I am forced to leave the court entirely to return a shot, and hit the shot around the net post rather than directly over the net? If the ball lands in your opponent's court you have made a fine shot.

A foot fault

What if the ball just barely touches me during a point? You lose the point.

What if you are playing someone who is obviously cheating you? The best solution is to not play with the person. There are other alternatives, however. You could request an umpire if it is a tournament match, or you could ask for a replay of a certain point.

I entered a tournament and had to play a very long match right off the bat. Luckily I won, but then the tournament director informed me that I could rest 15 minutes and then would have to play my second match. Is this legal? Unfortunately, yes. The usual practice, however, is to not require a person to play more than one match in the morning and one in the afternoon. Unfortunately, it does not always work out this way. Please read Chapter 13 on Conditioning for Tennis.

How much time do I have between games when changing ends of court? Technically, one and a half minutes. However, most people do not complain if you towel off, take a drink and wipe your glasses. They have a right to complain if you repair your racket or decide to change socks and shirt.

Tennis players should always be good sports, even when it's not easy!

I occasionally play indoors and my opponent's lobs sometimes hit the lights because of a low ceiling. He always insists on replaying the point. What should I do? He is flimflamming you. If a shot hits an obstruction, whoever hits the ball last loses the point.

In doubles, can my partner and I change sides of the court to receive a serve? No. You must wait until the beginning of a new set.

The person I compete with frequently "quick serves" me. What can I do? Quick serving is illegal. However, if you swing at the ball it is assumed you were ready. Do not swing at the ball; tell your opponent that you were not ready.

I sometimes play with this guy who is better than I am and he always wants to rally to see who serves first. If I were better than you and could get you to agree to this, I would too. Tell him the rules say to either spin or flip for choice of serve.

Another person I play with always wants to begin play on the "first serve in." Is this legal? No. All practice serves must be made before the first point is played.

My opponent hit a great shot but it buried itself under the net strap just below the top of the net. My opponent claimed he should have a replay because his topspin would have taken the ball over. I gave him another shot but I think I was taken. Was I? Yes, you were flim-flammed. Rule 17 says that a ball embedded in the net is out of play and the hitter loses the point.

Spinning the racket for choice of serve—up or down?

Can I serve the ball underhanded with lots of spin? Yes. Can I fake the underhand serve and then serve over-hand? Yes. There are no restrictions on preliminary motion once the receiver is ready for your serve.

Do I have the right to demand that my opponent remove a loose ball lying in his court? Yes, but at the appropriate time.

POINTS OF PLAYER AND SPECTATOR ETIQUETTE

1. Before beginning a match always introduce yourself to your partner and opponents.
2. Always check net height at the beginning of a match. One convenient way is to take two standard rackets and stand one end with the head of the other on top.
3. Take all practice serves before playing any points.
4. As a server, do not begin serving any point unless you have two balls at the ready.
5. Failure to observe the foot fault rule will cost you friends.
6. Call lets and faults out in a loud clear voice. A point of the finger upward or sideward will also reinforce a voice call.
7. Never "quick serve" an opponent.
8. Never give unsolicited advice and restrict comments to the conduct of the game.
9. Control emotions and temper.
10. If your ball rolls onto an adjacent court, wait until the point is over then shout, "Thank you, please?"
11. When returning a ball to players on another court, wait until their point is finished and they are looking at you.
12. Return only served balls that are good.
13. Do not make excuses. If you lose, you lose, and always shake hands with your opponent.
14. Do not lean on the net to retrieve a ball.
15. If you must cross an occupied court to reach yours, wait until their point or game has been completed; then go quickly to your court.
16. Hit any shot requested by your opponent during the warm-up period.
17. Do call a "let" whenever another ball enters your court and return it to its owner.
18. Do keep score accurately.
19. Do give the benefit of the doubt on close calls to your opponent.

21. Do dress properly according to local customs.
22. Do announce the score when you are serving.
23. Never boo a player.
24. Applaud good shots.
25. No moving while ball is in play (spectators).
26. No loud talking or yelling when ball is in play.
27. Do allow the umpire or players to call the match. They are in a much better position than you to call most shots.
28. Do not ask a spectator whether or not a shot was in or out.
29. Never hit a ball directly at an opponent except during official time in play.
30. Never monopolize the courts.
31. Never wear basketball or jogging shoes on a soft surface court.

TENNIS TERMS

ACE: A perfect serve that is hit beyond the reach of one's opponent.

AD: A shortened word for advantage which refers to the next point after the score is deuce.

AD IN: The score when a serving player wins the next point following deuce.

AD OUT: The score when the receiving player wins the next point following deuce.

ADVANTAGE: The next point after deuce.

ALL: Denotes a tie score as in 30-all, meaning 30-30.

ALLEY: A 4 1/2 foot lane on both sides of the singles court and necessary for doubles play.

AMERICAN TWIST: A type of topspin serve used mainly in doubles play. The topspin imparts a high bounce allowing the server more time to follow the serve to the net.

APPROACH SHOT: The shot which is taken just before the hitter moves into the net.

AUSTRALIAN DOUBLES: A formation in which the net person lines up on the same side as the server.

BACKCOURT: The court area between the service line and the baseline.

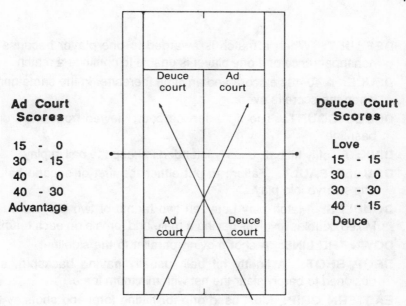

Ad Court
Scores

15 - 0
30 - 15
40 - 0
40 - 30
Advantage

Deuce Court
Scores

Love
15 - 15
30 - 0
30 - 30
40 - 15
Deuce

BASELINE: The back line or the farthest line from the net.

BASELINE GAME: One who rarely attempts to take the net or play in the forecourt.

BIG GAME: A style of play popularized by Jack Kramer and utilizing the hard serve, followed by a pressing net attack.

CARRY: An illegal shot causing the ball to be slung or hit twice before crossing the net.

CENTER MARK: A short perpendicular line which divides the baseline at its center.

CHOP: A downward stroke of the racket, usually causing the ball to rise slightly and, depending on the surface, to skid or bounce low.

CLOSED TOURNAMENT: An event open only to the member of a particular club or geographical area.

CONTINENTAL GRIP: A grip utilizing a position halfway between an Eastern forehand and classic backhand. The grip does not require a player to change grips for the forehand and backhand stroke.

CORE STRING: A very common and durable tennis string consisting of a single or multiple core surrounded by individual nylon fibers.

CROSSCOURT SHOT: When the ball is hit diagonally from one side of the court to the opposite corner on the other side.

DEFAULT: When a match is awarded to one player because of nonappearance or if one player is unable to continue a match.

DEUCE: A 40-40 tie score and anytime thereafter in the same game when the score is even.

DEUCE COURT: The right service court viewed from one's own baseline.

DINK: A softly hit ball, usually intended to keep the ball in play.

DOUBLE FAULT: Failure to put either the first or second ball of one's serve into play.

DOUBLES: Match play between two teams of two players each. Mixed doubles involves having a male and female on each team.

DOWN THE LINE: A shot moving parallel to the sideline.

DROP SHOT: A lightly hit ball, usually having backspin, and designed to barely clear the net with minimum force.

EASTERN GRIP: Most used grip for hitting forehand shots. Also called the "shake hands grip."

ELONGATION: The amount of potential stretch in a string. Present elongation in today's strings range from 5% to 18%.

FAST COURT: A smooth court surface causing the tennis ball to move quickly to the hitter.

FAULT: The failure to serve a ball within the proper service court.

FOOT FAULT: An illegal serve caused by the server stepping into the court as the racket makes contact with the ball.

GAME: One portion of a set which occurs when one person or team wins four points and are at least two points ahead. On tie games, i.e., 30-30 or 40-40, it is the first side to gain a two-point lead.

GAUGE: Represents the diameter of a tennis string. The thinner the string the higher the number. Strings usually run 15 to 18 gauge.

GRAND SLAM: A tennis achievement requiring the winning of the U.S. Open, The French Open, The Australian Open, and the Wimbledon all in the same year.

GROUND STROKE: A forehand or backhand stroke occurring after the ball has bounced.

GUT: Natural strips of sheep or cow intestine that are twisted and braided together to form a tennis string.

HACKER: A tennis player with limited form and skills.

HALF VOLLEY: A defensive shot usually occurring when the ball is hit halfway between a volley and a regular ground stroke. The ball is blocked or hit with a very short backswing just as it begins to rise from a bounce.

INVITATIONAL TOURNAMENT: Competition open only to players who receive the invitation.

ILTF: The International Lawn Tennis Federation.

LET: Whenever a point needs to be replayed. Generally it occurs when a serve hits the top of the net and lands in the proper service area.

LET SERVE: As above, but pertains only to the service.

LOB: A high soft shot usually used to drive's one's opponent back to the baseline, or to allow the hitter more time to assume better court position.

LOVE: Zero in tennis scoring.

MATCH: A tennis contest involving wither singles, doubles, or teams.

MATCH POINT: The final point needed to close out a match.

MONOFILAMENT NYLON: A relatively weak string using one strand of thick nylon which is lightly susceptible to changes in temperatures.

NET UMPIRE: When officials are employed, this person calls let serves.

NO OR OUT: The terms used by some players to denote a ball that did not land within the proper court area.

NO AD SCORING: A new version of scoring requiring the winner to have four points. If the score is tied at three all, then the next point determines the winner.

NO MAN'S LAND: The court area located between the baseline and the service line; generally considered to be a poor area to attack from or to defend.

OVERALL STIFFNESS RATING: Indicates "racket feel." A rating of 1-4 is usually very flexible. Ratings of 6-10 usually denote a stiff racket. Stiff rackets usually provide more power and consistency.

OVERHEAD: A free swinging hard shot usually very much like the serve.

PASSING SHOT: A ball hit low and hard to the side of a person who has moved in to "take the net."

POACH: Generally refers to the doubles play of a net person who is able to pick off shots intended for a partner.

POWER ZONE RATING: An area on the racket face usually located just below the sweet spot center. Balls striking above the power zone tend to lose power as they move nearer the top of the racket.

PRO SET: An abbreviated match which is completed when one player wins at least eight games and is ahead by at least two games.

PUSHER: A soft hitter who is generally very steady.

RALLY: An exchange of shots after the serve, usually from the baseline.

RECEIVER: The person who is to receive and return the serve.

RETRIEVER: A type of player who plays a defensive game and returns all shots.

SERVICE BREAK: The loss of a game by a server or a serving team.

SERVICE LINE: A line running parallel to and 21 feet from the net.

SET: A component part of a match which occurs when a player or side has won at least six games and is ahead by at least two games.

SLICE: To hit the ball with side spin and a slight undercutting motion.

SLOW COURT: A rough or soft surface court causing the tennis ball to "bite in" or to move more slowly to the hitter. Good examples of slow courts are clay and rubico (Har-tru).

SPLIT SETS: When both players or teams have won one set and the match outcome will be determined by the remaining set.

STRAIGHT SETS: To win a match without losing a set.

SUDDEN DEATH: When a tie breaker goes to the final point.

SWEET SPOT: The point on the racket face giving the least vibrations on ball contact.

TAKE TWO: Whenever the receiver indicates that the server should repeat two serves.

TENSILE STRENGTH: A measure of overall strength. Today's strings range from about 140 pounds to 220 plus.

TWISTED BUNDLES STRING: A modification of the twisted fibers string in which several bundles of twisted fibers are coated and encased in a urethane coating.

TWISTED FIBER STRING: A string made by twisting multiple nylon fibers and bonding them together with urethane.

USTA: An abbreviation for the United States Tennis Association.

VASSS: An abbreviation for the Van Alen Simplified Scoring System. A set is completed whenever one person scores 21 or 31 points.

VIRGINIA SLIMS: A series of tournaments or regular competition for female tennis players who are professionals.

VOLLEY: A short backswing shot taken before the ball hits the court. It is the primary weapon for doubles play.

WESTERN GRIP: A forehand grip which allows the hitter to impart severe topspin to the ball.

WORLD TENNIS TEAM: An organization composed of the world's best male and female professional players.

A. Scoring Problem for a Game

Point No.	A	B	Score
1	x		
2	x		
3		x	
4	x		
5		x	
6		x	
7	x		
8		x	
9		x	
10		x	

A=Server; B=Receiver

B. Scoring Problem for 12-Point Tie-Breaker

Point No.	A	B	Score
1	x		
2		x	
3		x	
4	x		
5		x	
6	x		
7	x		
8		x	
9		x	
10	x		
11		x	
12	x		
13	x		
14		x	
15	x		
16	x		

A is the first server and serves from the south side of the court.

QUESTIONS:

1. How many points were served by A? By B?
2. What was the final score in the set?
3. What was the final score in the tie breaker?
4. To which court was the 9th point served, right or left?
5. To which court was the 14th point served, right or left?
6. When the game was concluded, was the server serving from the north or south side of the court?
7. How many times did the players change ends of the court?
8. Which players will be serving the first point of the next set?

CHAPTER 3 EVALUATION

1. Name the points you may win in a game, using the correct scoring terminology. Begin with the first point you can win and proceed progressively to the final point.

2. Abbreviated scoring terminology is frequently and universally used. What are the terms generally used?

3. You must win by a minimum of _____ points and be at least _____ ahead to win a game.

4. The term "deuce" means that you and your opponent have each won at least _____ points.

5. What is the definition of a set? How do you win a set using conventional scoring? Using a tie breaker?

6. Explain how you win a match.

7. What is unique about the ninth point in the 9-point tie breaker?

8. If a ball in play partially touches the line, is it a good shot?

9. When is a point won by a player? How can your opponent lose the point in play? Name several ways.

10. On the toss of the coin for service, you win. What are your choices?

11. When do my opponent and I change ends of the court?

12. The ball was clearly out of bounds when I caught it in mid-air. It had not touched the court yet. Whose point?

13. What is the ruling if you think a ball is out, but you are unsure and there is no mark left by the ball?

14. How does the VASSS No-Ad scoring system differ from conventional scoring?

15. Who serves the first game of the next set following a 9-point tie breaker? A 12-point tie breaker?

16. The score is 40-15, which court does the server use for the next point?

17. A term used to describe a tie breaker that goes into the last point is?

18. Is the diagram for scoring problem A at the end of this chapter using conventional or No-Ad scoring?

Gripping the Racket

HITTING THE TENNIS BALL

Since most of you have probably received elementary tennis instruction and have played some tennis prior to reading this book, you know that the forehand drive is the "bread and butter" shot of the game. It is quite likely that since this stroke seemed easier to hit than the backhand, you favored the shot, and now find yourself playing three-quarters of the court with the forehand. You also may now pray that your opponent will not hit the ball down the line on the backhand side.

If this is the case, do not be unduly concerned since you must have a good forehand and the only way to acquire one is to practice hitting from that side. It does mean, however, that you must begin to hit a greater percentage of backhand shots; otherwise, the difference in the ability to hit both shots will appreciate even more, and you will become more vulnerable.

As with any endeavor there are certain generalizations or "principles" which, if applied, will improve performance. This does not rule out individual differences. However, if one studies the current greats in tennis, it will be quickly noted that most seem to have nearly identical form in their basic strokes.

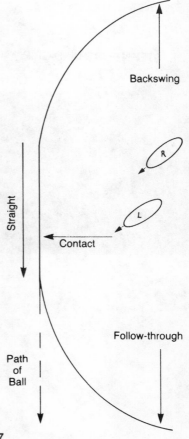

Racket path of forehand stroke
(top view)

FOREHAND GRIP

EASTERN

The Eastern grip is the most commonly used grip of tennis players. It is often called the "shake hands" grip since the racket handle is grasped as you would the hand of a friend.

The palm will be in the same plane as the face of the racket, and the heel of the hand will rest lightly against the butt of the handle. The fingers should be spread with the index finger spread slightly more than the others. This will cause a "V" (the junction of the thumb and index finger) to rest squarely on the top of the handle so that if a line were to be drawn from the "V" it would fall over the right shoulder.

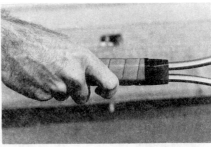

EASTERN FOREHAND GRIP

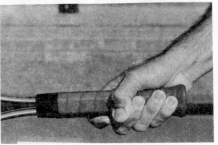

CONTINENTAL GRIP

The Continental is a grip that places the hand midway between the Eastern forehand and the Eastern backhand. The advantage is that no change has been made for forehand or backhand shots. Thus, this grip is sometimes favored by players who react slowly at the net, by players who volley a great deal, and by players who play doubles exclusively. The disadvantage is a slight reduction in hitting power and the necessity of a strong wrist.

To assume the Continental grip, move your hand around the handle to the left of the Eastern grip. The knuckle of your index finger will rest halfway between the top of the handle (as in the classic backhand) and the back of the handle (as in the Eastern forehand). Finger spread and thumb position is the same as the Eastern forehand. See illustrations below.

Side View   CONTINENTAL GRIP   Top View

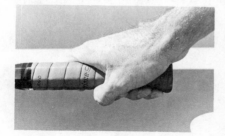

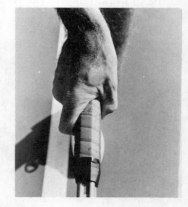

WESTERN GRIP

The Western grip is achieved by moving the hand in a clockwise direction from the Eastern grip, or hand shaking grip, so that more of the palm of the hand will be under the handle rather than behind it as in the Eastern. The racket hand rotates a quarter of a turn toward the bottom (clockwise) of the handle. This creates a closed face of the racket, more or less depending on the extent of the rotation.

Because this grip permits exaggerated topspin to be placed on the ball, it is becoming more popular with players due to the publicity given topspin by today's professional players.

One of the difficulties experienced by younger players lies in the low trajectory caused by this grip. The player must learn to adjust to an aiming point much higher than the Eastern forehand in order to clear the net. Another problem lies in the change from forehand grip to backhand grip. Due to the exaggerated turning of the hand in the Western forehand grip, the distance to the Eastern backhand is lengthy and, in a fast exchange, there may not be enough time to make the change. The Western grip is not recommended for beginners by the authors.

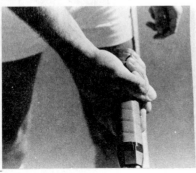

Top View

WESTERN GRIP

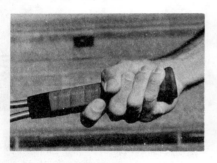

Rear View

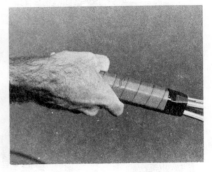

MOST COMMON ERRORS OF THE FOREHAND GRIP

1. The fingers are too close together resulting in a hammer grip.
2. The player grips the racket too tightly in between shots resulting in a hammer grip.
3. The grip is not firm enough at impact.
4. The index finger is not wrapped around the handle but rather points toward the head of the racket.
5. Improper angle of the wrist.

BACKHAND GRIP

THE EASTERN BACKHAND

One of the most common faults among beginners is the attempt to hit backhand shots without turning the racket. Unless the racket is turned it will be impossible to present the racket face perpendicularly to the ball and at the same time maintain a smooth fluid stroke.

To place the racket face in the desired position, you must turn the hand a quarter turn counterclockwise from the Eastern forehand grip. This will place the knuckle of your index finger **on top of the handle.** The thumb should be kept at a diagonal, but may be shifted upward slightly for additional support. The fingers should be spread slightly as in the Eastern forehand. For best results, turn the racket by simultaneously loosening the forehand grip and turning the throat of the racket with the left thumb and index finger. This should be done as the left hand is guiding the racket back into a full backswing.

EASTERN BACKHAND

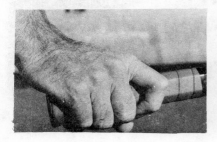

MOST COMMON ERRORS OF THE BACKHAND GRIP

1. Failure to change from the forehand grip.
2. Improper placement of the thumb or fore-finger.
3. Insecure grip at moment of impact.

THE TWO-HANDED BACKHAND

In the last several years a number of ranking tennis players have demonstrated that the Two-handed backhand can be a very effective weapon. Its advantage lies in allowing a person to hit with more power, in controlling the racket more effectively if the person is very small or weak, and providing a better opportunity to hit with topspin. Its chief disadvantage is that one cannot reach as far on wide shots as with the Conventional backhand.

To assume the Two-handed backhand grip, place your right hand in the same position as for the Eastern backhand. The left hand is placed in a position similar to the Eastern forehand, but just above and touching the right hand. Both hands should be placed on the grip at the beginning of the pivot turn and preparatory to the back-swing.

The right hand plays the dominant role with the left providing added wrist support, control, and power. Contact with the ball should occur as the ball reaches the front foot. Extremely wide shots may necessitate your releasing the racket with your left hand as you hit.

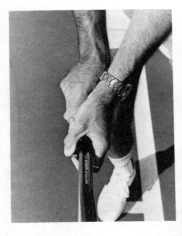

TWO-HANDED BACKHAND

Remember the relationship of the racket face to each type of grip:

Continental
The racket face is **open**

Eastern
The racket face is **flat**

Western
The racket face is **closed**

CHAPTER 4 EVALUATION

1. Contrast the Eastern, Western, and Continental grips.

2. List some of the more common errors associated with the Eastern Forehand grip.

3. What are some of the more common errors associated with the Eastern Backhand grip?

4. What are the advantages of the Two-handed Backhand vs the Conventional Backhand grip?

5. Why should the tennis stroke an serve exclude superfluous movement?

6. What is the relationship between ball spin and ball speed?

7. What are the advantages and disadvantages of using a Western grip? A Continental grip?

8. If a Two-handed grip is used, which hand might be considered dominant?

9. What is the position of the "V" formed by the thumb and fore-finger in the Eastern grip? In the Eastern Backhand grip?

10. The most popular grip by far is the _____.

   The grip that puts excess topspin on the ball is the _____.

   The grip that offers a "closed" face to the ball is the _____.

11. Which grip can be identified as the "shake hands" grip? How is it obtained?

12. What is the main universal problem with the Two-handed Backhand grip? How can this be overcome?

Principles of Stroking

SIMPLICITY

Most of you have probably heard the story of the man who was to deliver an important speech. His wife, while typing the speech, made a notation at the top of the page. The notation was in the form of the four letters KISS with an arrow drawn to the bottom of the page. At the bottom of the page were the words "Keep it simple, stupid."So the first principle of hitting the tennis ball is to "keep the stroke simple."

The authors once knew a fairly good player who swung at a tennis ball and hit himself in the mouth with his own tennis racket. The end result was eight stitches. Obviously he had not read this book and his stroke was not a simple stroke. The tennis swing is not a complicated windup with fancy gyrations as is sometimes seen. Rather it is a smooth, nearly effortless, and fluid motion which causes the head of the racket to increase momentum culminating on impact so that the total power of the swing is transferred into the tennis ball. One way to help develop this fluid swing is to stand in front of a mirror and simply "dry swing" your tennis racket while thinking of the various components that go to make up a good stroke.

As we look into the simplicity of the tennis stroke, we find that early preparation greatly contributes to our theory. Most of today's tennis teaching professionals will tell you that if you can eliminate those many unnecessary movements that tend to creep into a person's tennis stroke, you will be greatly rewarded by success.

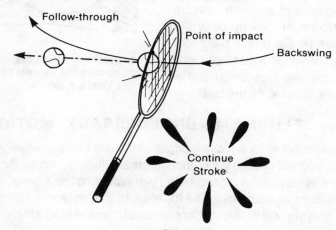

Follow-through

Point of impact

Backswing

Continue Stroke

The tennis stroke is basically a low to high trajectory. The purpose of the low to high stroke technique is to allow you to stroke the ball with sufficient height to clear the net, the cause of most of our errors. In utilizing the stroke, drop the head of the racket to a point slightly lower than, but in line with, the anticipated contact point of the ball. Don't add anything fancy to this backswing motion—just take the racket back. As the ball approaches, simply swing the racket into the ball, raising the racket into the follow-through. No excess motion of the feet, wrist or arm is needed.

Many times we tend to believe that we have to do something extraordinary to be successful. In tennis, the more unnecessary motions we eliminate, the better off we will be.

CONCENTRATION

It is quite probable that this principle, more than any other, separates the winners from the losers in tennis. When hitting the tennis ball you must drive all thoughts from your mind and concentrate almost entirely on watching the tennis ball. The vast majority of missed shots in tennis are due to the person making the shot while not totally watching the ball.

The principle also applies to other sports. Ted Williams, the famous baseball hitter, is attributed to having said that he always tried to follow the baseball with his eyes from the pitcher's hand to the moment of impact with his bat. One way to assist in the development of stroke concentration is to never look up until after you have hit the tennis ball. How often have you looked to see what your opponent was doing just as you were about to hit the ball?

Maintaining concentration separates the winners from the losers in tennis.

ELIMINATE UNNECESSARY MOTION

If you attempt to hit a moving target with a rifle or pistol while you are moving, you will probably experience great difficulty. However, if you stop or hesitate, even momentarily, you would notice a great deal of improvement in accuracy. The identical is true in tennis. Beginning tennis players will find great improvement in stroking ability if they cease moving just prior to hitting the ball.

Another problem frequently experienced by beginners is an unnecessary bending motion at the knees and hips, so that in addition to unnecessary lateral motion they also are bobbing up and down with the stroke. Many beginners also experience great difficulty because they loop their swing instead of bringing the racket back more in a straight line. If you are experiencing difficulty in hitting the ball, try repeating to yourself just prior to stroking the shot, **"Straight back — step swing."** At the same time, bring the racket hand back in a straight line at the expected bounce level for the shot being played.

Avoid unnecessary motion when you swing at the ball.

DEVELOP SMOOTHNESS OF MOTION

Do not be discouraged if you seem to appear and feel awkward the first few times you attempt a new stroke or new movement. Try to remember your first attempt at riding a bicycle. Repetition will increase your smoothness and ultimately your movements will become as "smooth as silk."

CONTROL

As a beginner your primary goal should be consistency and accuracy rather than speed or spin. To develop the "feel or touch" necessary for consistency, you should concentrate on hitting the ball with only moderate pace. In time you will gain confidence in your strokes, and will want to gradually increase the pace of your shots.

Spin is imparted to the tennis ball by the angle of the racket face at the moment of impact. The basic spin is a slight topspin created by starting the shot low and finishing high thus causing the ball to spin from top to bottom and resulting in a downward drop or curve in the flight of the ball.

BALANCE AND POWER

Balance is fundamental to all sports and tennis is not an exception. The ability to handle low shots and to move quickly in any direction necessitates that you be relaxed and with the knees slightly flexed.

Power is the force that is gained by the fine coordination of racket, arm, and weight transfer necessary to move the ball in the direction you wish to go. Early preparation is essential. Just as in softball where the batter steps into the pitch, you should step into the line of shot.

This is accomplished by transferring your body weight to the forward stepping foot, which is kept flat on the ground. The heel of the back foot is usually off the ground and bears little weight. The face of the racket then moves into and through the intended flight path of the ball. Additional power and a free swing will be possible if you are able to keep your waist relatively straight. However, remember that an increase in power can contribute to loss of control. So proceed with caution.

PREPARATION

Success in tennis certainly depends upon all of the aforementioned qualities. An understanding of them, and a ready application will greatly enhance your chances of winning and playing well. They will require much from you and demand many hours on the court, from both a mental and a physical nature.

Preparation is that additional ingredient that turns the difficult shot into an easy one. When the ball is hit by the opponent you have several things to evaluate, and little time to do it. They are:

— the speed of the ball (slow, medium, fast)
— the type of spin you have to contend with (topspin or backspin)
— the height of the ball (shallow or deep)
— the angle of the flight (close or wide)

Your quick adjustment to these factors will show itself in your ability to return the ball successfully. Ideally you should be ready to return the ball by the time the incoming ball strikes your court. This **preparation** will have you moving quickly to the ball, allowing sufficient time for the footwork and stroking sequences to occur. There is no substitute for early and proper preparation. Anticipation is the key to this problem. With serious effort in this direction, your game and success in stroking can improve rapidly.

WATCH THE BALL

No matter if you are beginning to learn the game or you are an experienced player, you must watch the ball. We all get distracted at times, and fail to concentrate on this key element of the game. You can't hit what you don't see. Try to watch the ball all the way to your strings. This will assure you of a stroke that contacts the ball correctly, in the center of the "sweet spot" of your racket. Try it—it works!

CHAPTER 5 EVALUATION

1. Which stroke principle is the most important as being the determining factor in winning or losing?

2. Most stroke errors are caused by a simple, easy-to-correct technique. What is it?

3. Why is it desirable to cease your movement pattern just prior to executing your tennis stroke?

4. How would you rank the following words — spin, power, speed, control, and accuracy? Explain why your ranking has been put in this order.

5. As a beginner, you should be primarily concerned with one characteristic. What is it?

6. The basic stroking technique will impart which type of spin on the ball?

7. An increase of power into the stroke can cause another problem. Name the problem.

8. How would you describe the simplicity of a tennis stroke? Begin from the ready position.

9. What is the key to preparation? What does it mean with reference to the game?

10. Explain where the power of a tennis stroke comes from.

11. What are the four factors you must contend with when you think about preparation? How can you solve the problems they present?

Footwork — Basic Patterns

As a beginner, intermediate or advanced player, you soon learn to realize that each stroke, whether it be a forehand or backhand, is very similar to the one preceding. The only difference is that the strokes may be made in different places. Hence the importance of footwork. It is most desirable to be able to move fluently and in a relaxed, controlled manner. Of all the ingredients of developing a successful and satisfying level of tennis, footwork is one of the most important. It has been said that footwork is 50 to 70 percent of the game. While this may be debatable, it certainly is a vital area that cannot be overlooked or taken lightly. As you observe a good player, you can easily see the relationship of footwork to stroke production and success.

Many inexperienced players appear to hit the ball in all sorts of positions. Most of these are uncomfortable, and the results are frequently unsatisfactory. Good footwork makes a difficult job easy. As stated earlier, most strokes follow the same basic technique — forehands are stroked about the same way each time, with slight adjustments. Backhands, volleys, etc., are the same. The difference in forehands may frequently be in footwork preparation.

The following explanations of proper footwork patterns will progress from simple to the complex.

THE READY POSITION

As a player begins to learn the game of tennis, he or she soon realizes that tennis balls cross the net at various speeds, angles and heights. It is infrequent that two shots in a row are the same. Thus, there is an immediate need to be continuously prepared, expecting everything. You may find yourself having to move quickly in any direction, covering half the court either on the forehand side or the backhand side. On the other hand you may have to move very little except to step forward and contact the ball. Alertness is the key!

73

The ready position is the stance used to facilitate quick movements. That is to say, the player can move in any direction, quickly and totally under control, whether the move is one step or a series of steps.

The ready position

In describing the ready position, we find the body is situated in the following manner. The racket is held comfortably, usually with an Eastern forehand grip. The other hand supports the racket, holding it loosely at the throat. The arms are usually close in to the body, supporting the racket at a position comfortably in front of the upper torso. The elbows are relatively close to the chest. The waist is slightly bent, allowing the body to bend forward comfortably, indicating a position of readiness. The knees are slightly flexed, with the weight evenly distributed on the balls of the feet. The feet are spread about shoulder-width apart. The keynote is comfort. In advanced tennis, it is not unusual to see the player receiving service jump slightly upon anticipating the contact of the ball on the server's racket. In fact, it probably happens more times than not.

THE FORWARD PIVOT

For balls close to the body — one step away.

Actually this footwork pattern may be done in three different ways, each correct and proper in its own style. Each style accomplishes the procedure of turning the body sideways to the net, allowing the racket to proceed into the backswing, and if completed properly, stepping into the stroke, thereby creating a weight shift into the flow of the stroke. The three variations are explained below.

The cross step pivot — This variation begins with the ready position. As the ball approaches the player, the player pivots on the ball of the right foot and steps across and slightly forward with the left foot. As the ball approaches the contact area, a slight weight shift is made as the racket moves into the ball. Upon the completion of the stroke, the weight is on the forward foot. The rear foot remains stationary. The toes are in contact with the ground, but the heel will be slightly raised.

This footwork pattern will remain the same for both the forehand and backhand stroke.

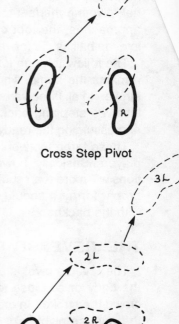

Cross Step Pivot

The turn and step pivot — This variation involves two separate movements by the player. As the ball approaches, the player merely turns the body to the side. There is no distinct footwork pattern, but a cross step may be used as discussed above. However, the forward foot will line up with the rear foot in a position approximately parallel to the net. The feet are kept close together. As the ball approaches, the player steps into the ball at a 45-degree angle, shifting the weight into the stroke as contact is made. The follow-through remains the same as in the cross step pivot.

Turn and Step Pivot

THE TURN AND STEP PIVOT

The twist and step pivot — The third variation is similar, yet quite different from the other pivot procedures. In this method the player, upon seeing the ball approach, simply turns sideways to the net, pivoting the feet to the side from the ready position. As the ball approaches, the foot closer to the net steps at a 45-degree angle into the ball as the forward swing is initiated.

The follow-through for this pivot, as in the others described above, remains the same. The weight is forward at the completion of the stroke. In all three variations the recovery to the ready position simply involves stepping back with the forward foot, again facing the net, and assuming the ready position.

These three footwork patterns will include many variations among players. Basically, however, the user will find that these three variations will more than suffice for stroking forehands and backhands with proper form. It should be noted that these same patterns are used with the backhand.

THE REVERSE PIVOT

The reverse pivot is used when the ball is coming either directly to the body or so close to the hitter that using a forward pivot would crowd the stroke. In order to properly position oneself for this stroke, the reverse pivot is used, starting with the basic ready position as shown. The following pattern is used for the right-handed hitter.

With feet in the ready position, begin your initial movement by a slight crouching movement in the knees. This is started as soon as the flight of the ball is determined. With the weight evenly distributed on the balls of both feet, simply pivot on the left foot, turning the body to face the forehand side as you step. Position the feet as shown in the illustration. Having positioned yourself thusly, put your weight once again on the right (rear) foot. You are now in a position very similar to those mentioned earlier under the forehand pivot.

THE REVERSE PIVOT

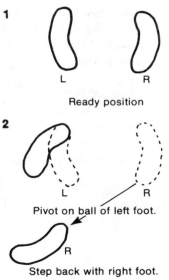

1

L   R

Ready position

2

L   R

Pivot on ball of left foot.

R

Step back with right foot.

As the ball approaches the contact area, with the weight comfortably on the rear foot, execute a forward step into the ball, as was done with the basic forward pivot. Very simply explained, you have just stepped back and away from the ball coming in too close to the body, and have placed yourself in a position so you can comfortably reach the ball and execute the stroke.

The reverse pivot is identical for the forehand and the backhand. The player will receive much benefit by starting early in preparing for the stroke.

THE SIDE-SKIP OR SHUFFLE STEP

This footwork pattern is used when the ball is away from the body—not close enough to be reached by a simple forward pivot. The side-skip pattern is a comfortable, easy movement that allows the body to pivot into the ball without breaking the flowing, rhythmical motion.

As with the other footwork patterns, the starting position in the ready position. As the ball is hit by the opponent, the footwork pattern should begin. This promptness is necessary because of the distance one must travel to get into position, and is complicated by the speed, depth and spin to the ball.

When moving to the right side, the first step is with the right foot. Initially, a slight crouch is taken by the player, and the weight is moved by pushing with the ball of the left foot, and stepping with the right foot to the side. The step should cover about three feet, or a distance that is comfortable for the player. When the right foot comes in contact with the court, the left foot follows and comes into place alongside, thus completing the first "step" of the side-skip pattern.

This pattern continues until the player is one skip or step away from the desirable pivot point. As the final step is made, the player begins a forward pivot into the ball, as explained earlier in the chapter. That is to say, on the last step, the right foot contacts the court and a pivot is made, pointing the right toe at a 45-degree angle to the net. As the

SERIES SHOWING SIDE-SKIP METHOD

Completed Stroke

weight is taken on the right foot, the left foot begins the step-across into the ball, continuing the 45-degree angle mentioned above. As the stroke is made, the weight will be maintained in the pattern outlined and no additional steps will be needed, except to recover into a ready position. However, this movement pattern is used to take the player away from the "home" position on the court, usually to the corners. It will be necessary to use it again to recover back to the center of the baseline (backcourt) area for the next stroke.

In moving to a ball that is either short in the court or to one that is deep, pushing you back away from the baseline, a short sidestep

OF FOOTWORK PATTERNS

Ready Position

motion is used, very similar to the step illustrated above. Short, quick steps are used rather than longer ones, as some adjustment will be necessary due to the low or high bounce. A player can greatly improve the situation by maintaining an alert, intense attitude. This will create a quicker initial response to each shot.

Finally, it should be noted that every player must frequently "run" to reach the ball. This happens when the player is too far from the ball and cannot otherwise reach the shot. However, upon reaching the ball, proper adjustments are necessary to create proper stroke footwork.

TIPS ON FOOTWORK

1. Keep a close watch on the ball to insure an early "jump" on the incoming shot. Begin your preparation as soon as the ball leaves the opponent's racket.

2. Anticipate where your opponent will hit each shot and begin moving early.

3. Look at the possible angles of return — to your right and left — now recover to the center of this angle.

4. When you contact the ball and return it to your opponent, recover quickly, as soon as your follow-through is completed.

5. In order to gain maximum benefit from your footwork pattern, your movement into the stroke should be rhythmical, relaxed, comfortable and *early*.

6. Be in position with racket cocked in the backswing *early*— this means no later than the bounce of the incoming ball

7. As you execute your stroke, keep the rear foot *in place* only allowing the weight to shift forward to the other foot. *Do not step* with the rear foot as the stroke is made.

8. Upon completion of your stroke, don't waste valuable time watching the shot, recover immediately.

9. Force yourself to think constantly about proper footwork procedures and movements. This will help you become more alert to the ball and your movement patterns.

10. Use a shuffle or side-step pattern to recover to your home position as this will be helpful in both preparation for the next stroke and in preventing the next ball from going "behind" you.

CHAPTER 6 EVALUATION

1. Describe the ready position.

2. Demonstrate the following: Cross Step Pivot, Turn and Step Pivot, Reverse Pivot and Side-Skip.

3. List 5 footwork tips.

4. Most receivers move slightly as the server contacts the ball. Why is this?

5. What grip is used when in the ready position? Why?

6. What is the purpose of the reverse pivot?

7. What part does good footwork play in the game of tennis?

8. Ideally, where should you strive to contact the ball?

9. What is anticipation? How can it assist you?

10. Which footwork pattern is used most to move side to side in the backcourt area?

11. Some players have their feet constantly in motion while awaiting the service, especially when the ball toss is made by the opponent. What advantage lies therein?

12. There are great similarities between the forward pivot and reverse pivot positions. What are they?

13. What are the advantages of using a 45-degree pivot instead of stepping directly forward or at a 90-degree angle to the incoming ball?

The Forehand

HITTING THE FOREHAND

Since we have previously discussed the Eastern grip and the ready position, we are now ready to proceed to a discussion of stroking fundamentals for the forehand drive.

BACKSWING

The backswing is started as soon as you see that the ball will land on the forehand side. Beginners will experience more success by drawing the racket back in a straight line until the head of the racket is pointing directly at the fence behind the baseline. This is accomplished by turning the left shoulder and moving toward the ball so that when the ball arrives, your early backswing will allow you time to adjust to unusual spin, speed, or bad bounce. As you acquire more experience, you will probably find yourself looping the racket head slightly in the form of an egg-shaped half arc.

THE BACKSWING

THE FOREHAND STROKE

Additional points of importance are:
— Stand straight from the waist up.
— The front knee should never be stiff.
— The toe of you back foot will be in contact with the ground but the heel will be off the ground.

IMPACT POINT

Impact Point

Whenever possible, you should hit the ball at waist level since this is the easiest and most effective point of impact. Should the ball be lower than waist level, lower the racket arm by bending the knees and not the back.

As your weight transfers to the front foot and the racket head moves toward the impact point, you should attempt to make contact with the ball slightly in advance of the front foot and beyond the midpoint of your body.

THE FOREHAND STROKE, *continued*

At the point of full backswing the racket head should be just slightly below the point at which you will hit the ball. This provides a low to high swing, which is necessary for imparting slight topspin to the ball. For low bouncing shots you must bend the knees and drop the shoulder farthest from the net. This will prevent the head on the racket from dropping below the handle and is very necessary for maintaining control.

We should note here that in the forehand stroke, the backswing does not utilize a straight arm or a locked elbow. The backswing is a relaxed comfortable reach behind the body, with the elbow about six to eight inches from the chest. The wrist is back to allow for a proper face on the ball at contact.

PIVOT AND MOVEMENT OF FEET

Your beginning position should be with the feet approximately shoulder-width apart, in the center of the court and one to three feet behind the baseline. As you move to the ball and stop at the desired position, your weight should be on the rear foot. The next movement is a step into the ball, much as a softball hitter does when stepping into a pitch. This transfers your weight into the line of shot and provides the power necessary for a successful stroke.

Follow-through

Follow-through is as important to tennis as it is to basketball shooting, throwing a football, or any other athletic endeavor involving hand-eye coordination. Perhaps the easiest way to develop follow-through is to establish checkpoints in your swing which, if adhered to, will guarantee that follow-through is taking place.

Follow-through Checkpoints:

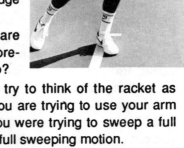

1. At the completion of your forward swing, is your front knee slightly bent with the ball of your foot in contact with the court?
2. Is the heel of your other foot (the back leg) slightly off the court at the conclusion of the swing?
3. Did you start the backswing low and finish in a high position — well out in front of your body and at least eye high?
4. Are you standing tall from the waist at the end of your follow-through?
5. Is the racket face still standing on edge at the end of your forward swing?
6. At the completion of your swing, are you looking over your elbow and forearm to where you want the ball to go?

When hitting the forehand, always try to think of the racket as being an extension of your arm. You are trying to use your arm and racket much as you would if you were trying to sweep a full table of dishes onto the floor in one full sweeping motion.

Remember to relax your grip between shots. Otherwise the muscles of your arm, hand, and wrist will experience early fatigue.

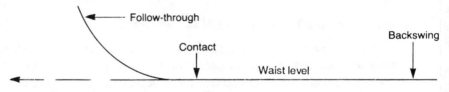

PATH OF FOREHAND GROUNDSTROKE

HITTING WITH TOPSPIN

Recent television coverage of tennis has created a desire by many players to develop topspin for both forehand and backhand shots. Many of today's top professionals use topspin with a high degree of success. To determine whether this method of stroking the ball is best for you, we must first examine the advantages and disadvantages before making a valid decision.

Advantages

— Topspin causes the ball to drop quickly to the court after clearing the net.
— The trajectory of a topspin drive will usually clear the net with greater height, thus resulting in fewer net errors.
— When returning a ball against a player at the net, the ball, if hit with a lower trajectory, will dip quickly, causing the opponent to return the ball upward.
— When used with proper depth, the opponent will either be forced to stroke the ball on the rise, or back up greatly to stroke the ball. Most players, unless highly advanced, will have difficulty doing this.
— A high topspin drive aimed toward the opponent's backhand creates a high bouncing shot, thus causing a very difficult return.

Disadvantages

— The player usually changes from the Eastern grip to the Western, causing an unfamiliar face on the racket.
— The footwork pattern of the player will change, causing the player to open the stance for the topspin drive.
— The body will face the net more, creating a change in technique.
— Most players return the ball short thus giving the opponent the chance to come to the net.
— The exaggerated low-to-high arm movement may contribute to arm and shoulder problems.
— Many hours of practice will be necessary.

A common problem in changing to the topspin stroke will be the immediate lack of control in directing the stroke. This is due mainly to the new angle of the racket face. The closed face caused by the Western grip will cause many balls to be hit into the net. In order to counter this problem, the player must adjust the aiming point of the stroke into a higher level above the net.

THE GRIP

Since most topspin players will use the Western grip, or a modification, a quick review of Chapter 4 should help to refresh your memory of the grip. Remember to turn your hand one quarter turn underneath the handle from the standard Eastern grip.

FOOTWORK

The footwork technique will change slightly, in that your stance will still allow you to stroke upward on the ball more aggressively to create the topspin. Some players stand facing the net when contacting the ball, and have excellent results.

At point of contact, the left foot is in front of the body, pointing generally at the net, the right foot is behind in a comfortable position (see diagram on the opposite page).

HITTING THE BALL

As the ball approaches, assume the correct grip and take your racket back as early as possible. Drop the head of the racket well below the intended contact point of the ball, and as the ball approaches, swing the racket forcefully upward using a sharp low to high trajectory. Since most players hit the ball using an aggressive pace on the racket head, the strings apply an excessive amount of topspin on the ball.

The follow-through continues upward to a point slightly past the height of the head of the player. Recovery to a ready position must be quickly made to prepare for the next return.

TOPSPIN STROKE SERIES

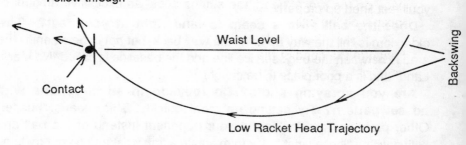

Follow-through

Waist Level

Backswing

Contact

Low Racket Head Trajectory

PATH OF TOPSPIN FOREHAND SWING

MOST COMMON FOREHAND ERRORS

Do you often hit the ball long? If you are consistently hitting balls long it may be because your opponent is hitting the ball hard. Do not try to hit with a slugger. Use the opponent's speed by shortening your backswing and letting the ball ricochet off your racket. Another possibility is that the face of your racket is open or tilted too far up. Or you may be allowing the ball to descend too far on the bounce before hitting. Try to take the ball at its highest point of bounce and bring the racket head back on a higher plane.

Do you often hit short or hit weak shots? The lack of hitting power usually results whenever you do not step into the ball and do not shift your weight with each shot. Are you following through on each shot and does the racket head finish well in front of the body? You may be delaying the swing and allowing the ball to get past you. Move your impact point forward. Late hits are sometimes caused because you do not begin the backswing soon enough.

Do you consistently hit shots to the right (right handers) or to the left (left handers)? It is likely that either your feet are lined up improperly or you are swinging late. Practice hurrying the backswing and try to move your impact point in front of the midpoint of your body.

Are you hitting the ball consistently to the left or "pulling the ball"? In this case you may be hitting too soon or you may not have your feet lined up properly.

Does the ball always seem to land right at your feet? The old axiom is "all the way up or all the way back, but not in between." The area is between the back service line and the baseline is called "No Man's Land" and is a poor place to be caught.

Are you spraying shots? Do they go in all directions with no set pattern? Try setting up more quickly. This means "hustle." Other problems are looking at your opponent instead of the ball and hitting with a "loose wrist." Try to maintain a firm wrist and do not try to hit either a raquetball, table tennis, or badminton shot. Good tennis requires a wrist that is a little more firm than any of the other mentioned sports.

Do you often hit the ball off center? If this happens frequently, the usual remedy is to watch the ball more closely. Failure to watch the ball "into the racket" causes the ball to occasionally hit on the frame of the racket or on the side of the face. This causes inaccurate shots and frequent errors. Early preparation and keeping your eye on the ball are the cures for the problem.

CHAPTER 7 EVALUATION

1. What is the reason for the grip on the forehand stroke? Point out the differences in hand positions and the resulting changes in stroke technique as compared to the backhand.

2. How soon should you begin your footwork preparation for the forehand stroke? Where will you want to hit the ball (contact point) in reference to your body if you have a choice?

3. Name the three grips recommended for use in the forehand stroke. How do they differ?

4. The vast majority of players will use the Eastern forehand grip. What are the advantages of using this grip compared to the others?

5. What is your "home position"?

6. List and explain the three basic parts of the forehand stroke.

7. What is the importance of the follow-through? What purpose does it serve?

8. At the completion of the stroke, where are the feet placed and how is the weight distributed?

9. What corrections would you make if you are consistently hitting the ball long? Why is this problem caused?

10. Why will you need to lay the wrist back in your backswing when executing a forehand stroke?

11. What is the problem when you are consistently stroking the ball to the right side of the court out of bounds?

12. At which height should the racket be taken in the backswing? Describe the path of the racket coming into the ball.

13. Where is "No Man's Land"? Explain the problems of playing here.

14. Many balls are hit off center, and not on the "Sweet Spot." What can you do to solve this problem?

15. Draw a line representing the directional flow of the head of your racket. Where, along this line, will you contact the ball. Why? What factors are involved?

16. Topspin users are very frequent in the game today. How does the grip and stroke change from the basic forehand?

17. What face is on the racket when topspin is used?

FOREHAND CHECK LIST

NAME _____ *P* = Poor *F* = Fair *G* = Good

Using another player to rally with your partner, check the appropriate letter as you observe your partner demonstrate his/her ability to use the forehand stroke. Allow appropriate warm-up time to determine accuracy in your observations.

1. The player utilizes the correct grip, or a slight variation of it.   P   F   G
2. Anticipation is good, allowing sufficient time to move to the ball.   P   F   G
3. Proper footwork is used in moving on the court.   P   F   G
4. Footwork is efficient — no wasted steps.   P   F   G
5. Player steps into the ball with the right foot as contact is made.   P   F   G
6. Backswing is taken back early — is not rushed.   P   F   G
7. Topspin and/or slice is used effectively during the stroke.   P   F   G
8. Racket swing is relatively level into the incoming ball.   P   F   G
9. Contact with the ball is made in front of the left foot.   P   F   G
10. There is little or no wrist evident in the entire stroke.   P   F   G
11. The follow-through begins immediately as contact is made.   P   F   G
12. The follow-through flows smoothly to the completion of the stroke.   P   F   G
13. The racket head is high and in front of the left shoulder at finish.   P   F   G
14. Recovery is rapid, awaiting the next shot.   P   F   G

COMMENTS (use reverse side if needed)

Chapter 8

The Backhand

To many people, the backhand is the most difficult stroke in tennis. To others, it is the strongest stroke. The difference probably is in the dedication and determination of the player to learn the fundamentals of the backhand, and then to practice enough to groove the shot.

Due to the necessary grip change, the backhand sometimes feels insecure, and it is easily understood that a sense of weakness might occur. Understanding the proper technique of the stroke will overcome most of these fears, and provision of enough practice time will generate sufficient confidence in the backhand.

CHANGING THE GRIP

The Eastern forehand grip, used by the vast majority of players, is the most comfortable grip known in tennis. It is easy to understand why it is so popular. The "shake hands" grip is easy to obtain, comfortable to hold, and blends well with the physics of technique. However, it is not a proper grip for the backhand. This is due primarily to the required change in the angle of the face of the racket.

The grip change from the Eastern forehand to the Eastern backhand simply involves a rotation of the hand one quarter turn counterclockwise (to the left) on the handle. This will make the following checkpoints:

— The racket face will become flat, allowing more hitting area for the ball.

— The "V" formed by the thumb and forefinger will be on the top of the left bevel on the handle.

— The large knuckle of the forefinger will be atop the top forward bevel of the handle.

— The fingers will remain spread to allow more control along the entire racket handle.

— The palm of the hand, if opened, will face down toward the ground.

— The thumb will comfortably lie alongside the handle, diagonally across the rear facet — not with the "thumbprint" on the facet.

95

Backswing   Contact (Side View)   Contact (Rear View)   Follow-through

THE BACKHAND STROKE

Finish high!

It should be emphasized that *wrist action* be kept to an *absolute minimum*. The less wrist the better.

Although this grip will be less comfortable initially to the player, constant use will generate a positive attitude toward the change, and a vast improvement in the game.

The change from the forehand grip to backhand grip usually occurs as the ball is traveling toward the player. Most players, in the ready position, will use a forehand grip while waiting for the ball. As the ball approaches toward the backhand, however, the change becomes necessary. While moving the body for proper stroke alignment, simply change from the forehand to backhand grip, supporting the racket with the other hand at the throat.

THE BACKSWING

As the ball approaches, the body is moving into position using proper footwork procedures. When the body begins to turn to the side, the grip change should be completed. Usually a player will keep both hands on the racket — one on the handle, and one supporting the racket along the throat during the backswing.

Ideally, the ball should be timed so that it is struck at a level between the knee and the waist—in the general area of the hip or thigh. Therefore, the backswing should be taken back at the same height as the anticipated contact point—hip high.

As the racket is taken back, the racket arm tends to straighten, allowing the handle to stay down at the level of contact. That is, the racket hand is down below the waist. The support arm, along the throat of the handle, is also kept relatively straight. This causes the racket to remain parallel to the ground throughout the backswing, and the face of the racket perpendicular to the court.

The length of the backswing will differ depending on the speed of the incoming ball and the quickness of the player. Usually a full back-swing is desirable, taking the racket back just past a line of 180 degrees or perpendicular to the net.

The wrist is kept firm throughout the entire backswing procedure and the grip is kept tight along the handle of the racket. Caution should be used to maintain a *level* backswing. The player should not lift the racket head or drop it downward as the initial backswing movement is started. An important reminder is that the racket should be taken back on a plane level with the anticipated contact area. Remember that the ball will come at various heights, causing some backswing movements on a low level and others at a high level. Fortunately, most are in the center of the extremes. The basic keys to success are (1) watching the ball closely and (2) getting an early start in your backswing preparation.

THE CONTACT AREA

When hitting a ball using the backhand stroke, we must remember that the ball contacts the racket six to eight inches in front of the forward foot. That is to say, the racket is further "toward the net" than in the forehand.

As the ball approaches, the racket begins its forward motion toward the ball. The hand tightens on the racket handle and the arm becomes firmer as the forward motion of the racket continues. It is necessary to make the wrist as strong as possible to absorb the impact of the ball.

An important criterion for a successful stroke is to be certain that the head flow of the racket leads the way into the ball. In other words, it does not trail the wrist and arm action moving forward. Rather, the arm, wrist and racket flow as one smooth pattern in a straight path. The major strength for the movement pattern is from the shoulder.

A major effort should be made by the player to keep the shoulders level with the court throughout the entire stroke. This will eliminate the common error of raising the shoulder of the racket arm on contact, causing the ball to fly on an upward trajectory and frequently go out of bounds.

As the motion flows from the backswing into contact of the ball, a strong effort should be made to keep the stroke in a level, "parallel to the court" pattern. The level path of the racket will allow maximum head contact with the ball, providing a drive that goes relatively deep into the opponent's court, and will create a slight amount of topspin to bring the ball down on the court.

Since the contact point is being made six to eight inches in front of the body, maximum use can be made of the forward shift of weight into the ball. However, care must be observed to keep from lifting the ball. As the racket meets the ball, the hitter should drive through the ball to establish a definite drive pattern — usually four inches to six inches will suffice.

THE FOLLOW-THROUGH

The follow-through is, in reality, the guidance system for the stroke. For example, if the follow-through is low, the ball will stay low. If it is straight, the ball does not clear the net, but usually will hit near the net cord.

Proper follow-through begins at the conclusion of the contact with the ball, and is a smooth upward flow of the racket. Please note that sufficient upward movement should be started while the racket is on the approach to the ball — or contact area. The follow-through seems to lift the ball over the net in the direction aimed by the racket. Remember this chart when you are swinging from low to high through the stroke:

Low Follow-through — Ball stays low (into the net).

Level Follow-through — Ball stays at the same height.

High Follow-through — Ball goes over the net.

This works, of course, if other things are also done correctly.

The desired direction of the ball is determined from the direction of the racket head at contact. If the desired flight is crosscourt, then the upward motion of the racket head is crosscourt. If you desire the ball to go down the line, then the upward motion is down the line, etc. This is the basic pattern for aiming the ball, and it works.

The player should note that the wrist is kept firm throughout the follow-through and the racket arm is kept straight in order to give proper guidance to the ball. This will greatly aid in controlling the stroke.

THE TWO-HANDED BACKHAND

The two-handed backhand is probably the latest innovation in tennis. Although it is not new, the two-handed stroke has recently become very popular. This is possibly due to the fantastic successes of some of the world's leading players such as Chris Evert, Jimmy Connors, and Harold Solomon. This trend is not without some justification, however. For example, a youngster just learning the game at age ten will definitely find strength a problem in using one hand for the backhand. At early stages of development, the wrist, grip, and arm are not strong enough to adequately control the racket upon impact with the ball, thus the two-handed stroke becomes a means to a successful end.

Although there are reach limitations in this stroke, proper footwork will overcome the problem. The user of the two-handed stroke should be very conscious of developing proper footwork patterns and the necessity of using them for each stroke. There is no substitute for good footwork.

Which grip(s) to use is sometimes a complex question. However, there is a relatively simple answer. The hitter has two choices:

1. The normal racket hand will use a correct *Eastern backhand* grip, and the support hand will complement this using an *Eastern forehand* grip. See Chapter 4.
2. Use two Eastern forehand grips.

The player may experiment with either of these two; however, the authors feel that the grip illustrated below left is the most comfortable. Support for this stems from the idea that if the learner is young, and strength is developed, there will possibly be a tendency to move on to a one-hand stroke. In such case, the proper grip will have been learned.

THE TWO-HANDED GRIP

Basic techniques for the stroke will follow the normal pattern explained earlier. To achieve satisfaction in consistency, accuracy and pace, early preparation and proper footwork, combined with the appropriate backswing, level stroke, and fluid follow-through, are essential. Dedicated practice will be the primary keynote to success.

There is one certainty: the shot is here to stay! There are too many world class players using it to be otherwise. So we have listed the plus and minus features and you make the choice.

+ Provides more topspin and power
+ Better for baseline players
+ Provides powerful service returns
+ Better suited for younger and /or weaker players

- Less reach than the one hand
- More difficult to volley coming in to net
- Difficult to volley a shot hit to one's middle
- Demands more exact footwork
- Difficult to slice or chop ball for backspin

TIPS ON TECHNIQUE FOR THE BACKHAND

1. Get ready early with proper footwork and backswing.
2. Keep your eye on the ball.
3. Turn the right side toward the net.
4. Change your grip as you pivot.
5. Take the racket back waist high.
6. Keep the racket arm relatively straight.
7. Step into the ball with the right foot as you stroke.
8. Contact the ball in front of the right side.
9. Lead with the head of the racket.
10. As you stroke, be relaxed as you swing.
11. Keep your stroke **level** until the follow-through.
12. Stroke through the ball and up in the follow-through.

Ready position   Beginning backswing   Full backswing

THE TWO-HANDED BACKHAND

MOST COMMON BACKHAND ERRORS

Contacting the ball late—behind the forward foot.
Begin your preparation earlier, as soon as the ball leaves the racket of your opponent. Watch the ball closely — anticipate the probable direction of the ball. Have racket back at full backswing position by the time the ball bounces.

Too much wrist used. As the pivot is made, tighten the grip on the handle, straighten the arm, and strengthen the wrist. Begin forward movement early, leading with the racket head. This is done by turning the entire arm into the stroke.

Leading with the wrist or elbow. This common error is corrected by mentally preparing early for the stroke, and concentrating on allowing the racket head to lead the way into the hit. Stroke with the shoulder and weight shift rather than just an arm and wrist movement. Keep the arm, wrist, hand and racket in a straight line as the stroke is made.

Trajectory is too low. Follow-through is low, or begins too late. As soon as the hit is made in front of the body bring the racket head up sharply into the desired direction.

Contact   Follow-through

THE TWO-HANDED BACKHAND, *Continued*

Trajectory is too high. Too much wrist used in the stroke, thereby accelerating the racket head as contact is made or the ball is hit, the shoulder is lifted upward, causing the flight of the ball to angle up. A high trajectory can also be caused by opening the face of the racket as contact is made. Correction is made by flattening the face of the racket somewhat.

Too much topspin. Improper face on the racket (closed) at contact, or the trajectory of the forward movement of the racket into the hit is improper. This is usually caused by either dropping the racket head initially or swinging upward at a sharp angle into the ball. Wrist becomes a problem here also. Level out the stroke, as explained earlier, and correct the racket face.

Ball pulls to the right (crosscourt) excessively. Caused primarily by poor footwork. Adjust stance and timing. Contact ball six to eight inches in front of body. Allow follow-through to only extend in the desired direction.

SKILLS PROGRESSIONS
FOR FOREHAND AND BACKHAND

REPETITIONS	DRILLS
5	1. From a ready position, obtain the correct grip. Release. Repeat.
10	2. From a ready position try the forward pivot, check foot position, recover.
10	3. Repeat No. 2 above using the reverse pivot.
10	4. Using the forward pivot, take the complete backswing. Check the height of the racket head.
10	5. Using the forward pivot, combine the backswing, forward swing, and the follow-through in one smooth motion.
25	6. From the back of the court, drop a ball in front of the desired side and stroke the ball into the fence 20 feet away. Recover to the ready position. Repeat.
30	7. Have a partner toss from the net (center) to the center line. Stroke using full pivot.
30	8. Toss from the net into the backcourt area (use a target) and stroke from the baseline into the opponent's court. Use full pivot.
15	9. Tosser will bounce and stroke a ball from the service line to partner at baseline on opposite side of the net. Pivot and stroke the ball back toward the tosser.
15	10. Hitter either drops ball or hits tossed ball into target area. (See diagram for accuracy drill.)

IF A REBOUND WALL IS AVAILABLE

25	11. Drop a ball as in #6 and stroke it to a rebound wall. Catch the ball, drop and repeat.
20	12. Repeat #10, keeping the ball to the right half of the forward rebound wall. The net line should be observed.

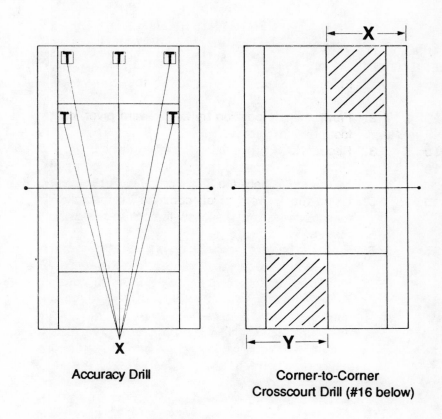

Accuracy Drill

**Corner-to-Corner
Crosscourt Drill (#16 below)**

20	13.	Repeat #11, keeping the ball to the left half of the forward rebound wall. Observe the net line.
30	14.	Try to replay the rebound against the forward wall. (Number of bounces is not important at this stage.
30 min.	15.	Drop a ball and stroke to your partner on the opposite side of the net. Try to continue as a rally.
	16.	X and Y keep the ball in play with a rally to the shaded areas shown on the court. Cover the area using backhand strokes only.

CHAPTER 8 EVALUATION

1. Describe the change from the Eastern forehand grip to the Eastern backhand.

2. Discuss the check points of an Eastern backhand swing, i.e., backswing, contact point, and follow-through.

3. Discuss three common errors of the backhand stroke and give directions for their remedy.

4. Diagram five drills suited to the development of a strong backhand.

108

5. Give reasons for the popularity of the two-handed backhand stroke. What are the major advantages? Disadvantages?

6. Explain the grips used in the two-handed backhand stroke. Which seems to be the favorite, and why?

7. Why is it felt that the backhand is the most natural of the ground strokes? Why do some feel it is the most difficult?

8. Name some of today's outstanding players who are proponents of the two-handed backhand.

9. Define the contact point for the backhand. How far in front of the body should the ball be hit?

10. What is the importance of the wrist in the backhand? How does this aid in control and consistency?

BACKHAND CHECK LIST

NAME _____   P = Poor   F = Fair   G = Good

Using another player to rally with your partner, circle the appropriate letter as you observe your partner demonstrate his/her ability to use the backhand stroke. Allow appropriate warm-up time to determine accuracy in your observations.

1. The player utilizes the correct grip, or slight
    variation of it.   P   F   G
2. Anticipation is good, allowing sufficient time
    to move to the ball.   P   F   G
3. Proper footwork is used in moving on the court.   P   F   G
4. Footwork is efficient — no wasted steps.   P   F   G
5. Player steps into the ball with the right foot as
    contact is made.   P   F   G
6. Backswing is taken back early — is not rushed.   P   F   G
7. Topspin and/or slice is used effectively during
    the stroke.   P   F   G
8. Racket swing is relatively level into the
    incoming ball.   P   F   G
9. Contact with the ball is made in front of
    the right foot.   P   F   G
10. There is little or no wrist evident in the
    entire stroke.   P   F   G
11. The follow-through begins immediately as
    contact is made.   P   F   G
12. The follow-through flows smoothly to the
    completion of the stroke.   P   F   G
13. The racket head is high and in front of the right
    shoulder at the completion of the stroke.   P   F   G
14. Recovery is rapid, awaiting the next shot.   P   F   G

COMMENTS (use reverse side if needed):

The Serve

Maurice McLaughlin set the tennis world on its ear in 1912 with a blistering serve that eventually won him the coveted U.S. Championship. Since that time, other tennis greats such as Pancho Gonzales, Roscoe Tanner, John McEnroe, Ivan Lendl, Boris Becker and Andre Agassi have decisively demonstrated that a tennis ball can be hit at speeds upward of 130 miles per hour and that the serve is the primary weapon of attack. Tennis authorities believe the serve to be the most important stroke of the game!

THE SLICE SERVE

The slice serve is very important to all tennis players. Since the ball has both side spin and underspin it is very difficult for an opponent to return this serve with excessive speed or precision. Hence, it is heavily relied upon as a second serve when the ball must be placed in play. To hit the serve, place the racket grip in a Continental position (halfway between forehand and backhand). Your front foot should be at a 45-degree angle and approximately 2-3 feet from the center mark.

STANCE

Your initial position for serving (in singles play) should be a position two to four feet from the center mark. This permits you to bisect the angle of the return of serve, thus equalizing the distance required to move for your return. Your feet and body should be in a throwing or hitting stance with the front toe at a 45-degree angle, about two inches behind the service line, and on a line parallel to the intended path of the ball.

Stance

THE SLICE SERVE

One necessary adjustment is to shift your toes so they are pointing at the right net post. Advanced players sometimes prefer to have both feet more parallel to the service line since this affords greater opportunity to uncoil the hips as the ball is being hit. If you continue to serve the ball too far to the left from this position even after adjusting your aim and wrist movement, you may need to move your rear foot slightly back and to the rear of the front foot. This places your non-hitting shoulder more sideways to the net and should move the ball to the right.

Your stance should be reasonably wide, at least shoulder-width, since this allows you to shift your weight to the back foot on the backswing and to the front foot during contact with the ball. As the toss is made, the rear foot should slide forward allowing a little more racket on impact with the ball.

At the moment of impact the body should have enough lean and forward momentum that to keep from falling on your face, the rear leg must be brought forward to support your body weight.

Remember to keep the front toe in contact with the ground throughout the toss and serving. This will insure that you do not foot fault and also will provide a firm support base for hitting.

THE TOSS

Two balls should always be in possession of the server on the first serve of every point. The ball being hit should be pushed into the air (not thrown) to a height equal or slightly greater than can be reached with the racket arm fully extended. It can not be stressed too highly that serving faults are almost always caused by an **inaccurate ball toss;** thus it becomes most important that you learn to toss the ball exactly where you wish it to go at all times. The toss should be made so that the ball is thrown to a height at least the distance of a fully-extended racket arm, and if allowed to drop, it should land about one foot to the right of your front toe and about one foot inside the court. This toss, which is slightly to the right of your body, will insure that sufficient slicing of the ball can occur. If the toss is not to the right it will be nearly impossible to impart the side-spin, slicing action necessary to the serve.

The serve itself is generally broken down into three phases — the toss and backswing, the forward swing, and the follow-through.

1. **The backswing.** The tossing arm and racket arm should begin the serve at least waist high with the ball hand touching the racket head. (See photos, next page.) As the left arm goes up, the racket arm drops down in a scissors or rocker motion, with the edge of the racket face leading. As the ball is released, the racket head begins an arc which brings it to a position behind the server's back with the elbow and wrist not yet cocked or bent. At this point the elbow and wrist begin to cock, allowing the racket head to move to a downward position almost touching the middle of the server's back.

2. **The forward swing.** As the ball descends the body weight shifts to the front foot, while the trunk and shoulders begin a forward rotation. As the wrist and elbow snap forward, the racket arm is fully extended at point of impact. The motion is often compared to throwing a ball or throwing one's racket into the proper service area.

3. **The follow-through.** The follow-through is simply a continuation of the forward swing making sure that the racket head ends up on the opposite side of your body and that the wrist fully uncocks so that it is pointing in the direction of the fence behind you and slightly downward. The right or back foot will cross the baseline to assist in maintaining body balance.

MOST COMMON ERRORS OF SLICE SERVE

1. The ball is not thrown as high as can be reached with the extended racket arm.

2. The ball is not hit at the full extension point, but is allowed to drop a foot or more before hitting.

3. The ball is not thrown far enough to the right to allow the necessary slicing action.

4. The wrist and elbow are not fully cocked. The check point is "scratching the back."

THE FLAT SERVE

Most professionals rely upon the Eastern grip to hit the flat, or no-spin serve. As the name implies, the ball is hit with the racket face square to the ball as opposed to attempting to cut off the right hand corner as in the slice serve. The old axiom, "less spin more speed," certainly holds true here. The two serves might also be compared with throwing an overhand fast ball and a semi-sidearm curve. The key factor in causing the racket face to meet the ball squarely is the angle that you cock your wrist. If the wrist is bent straight back and brought straight through, then the ball will be hit with little or no spin. On the other hand, if you cock your wrist at an angle and snap through with a twist, as a curve ball pitcher does, then you will impart a slicing or spinning motion to the ball.

Whereas the flat serve is very effective for reasonably tall — six feet or over — players, most short players will probably have more success with the slice serve. Remember also that to hit the flat serve the ball must be tossed more off the left toe and not as far to the right as in the slice serve.

THE AMERICAN TWIST SERVE

The American twist or topspin is probably the toughest serve to master since it requires an unnatural arm motion. Its value lies in its use as a second serve which has a high kicking action into the opponent's backhand, and for doubles play, since the high bounce allows the server more time to come in behind the serve.

To execute the serve, place the racket in an Eastern backhand grip. The ball must be tossed slightly behind the body and in back of the head. As the racket face moves to make contact, the server must hit up on the ball and at the same time snap the wrist hard over top of the ball. Since the ball is tossed slightly behind the body, this will cause the server to bend backwards more, but will also cause an upward hitting motion. The impact point on the tennis ball should be at least 10 or 11 o'clock and with a topward rolling wrist motion. This motion resembles a brushing upward movement on the back of one's head. The follow-through is to the right side of the body.

THE FLAT SERVE

THE AMERICAN TWIST SERVE

THE FLAT SERVE *continued*

THE AMERICAN TWIST SERVE, *continued*

PRACTICE HINTS FOR SERVING

1. Move in about halfway to the net and practice throwing a tennis ball into the proper service area. Throw vigorously using considerable wrist snap.

2. Now throw for the corners of the service area.

3. Gradually move back until you are on the baseline.

4. Practice the serving motion in front of a mirror. If the ceilings are too low use a table tennis paddle as a substitute for your racket.

5. Take a basket of balls and back off from the fence approximately 38 feet. Mark the fence either with an imaginary three-foot high line or attach several pieces of white tape in a line. Serve over the tape.

6. If you are having trouble serving from the baseline, move in about halfway — to the back service line. As speed and accuracy improve gradually back away until you are again behind the baseline.

7. Place racket covers or empty ball cans in critical serving areas and attempt to hit them with your serve.

8. The most important thing is to carry a basket or sack of old balls with you each time you go to the courts. Before leaving, always hit at least one sackful.

9. If you are having trouble synchronizing your toss and backswing, try tossing with the racket already cocked behind your back. Remember to take it all the way back to the "backscratching" position. Also, remember that this procedure is only a temporary measure and that eventually it will be to your advantage to take a full windup.

TIPS ON SERVING

1. Take your time when serving. Plan the type of serve you wish to use, and select the area of the receiving court you intend to hit the service into. Don't rush! Perhaps bouncing the ball 3 to 4 times will help you to prepare yourself.

2. Position yourself properly at the baseline — and don't change your basic position if using a different type of service. Otherwise, you may tip off the service you intend to use.

3. Be constant in your racket swing. This motion should be correct each time. The racket should not vary, since you maintain a firm grip on it.

4. Raise the elbow to allow smooth drop of the racket head behind the back. This does wonders to help solve this problem area.

5. Practice enough to regulate your toss. The important aspects are ball position, height and direction. You cannot adjust properly for a poor toss!

6. Practice reaching upward to hit the ball. That is, reach up to make contact. Hit with an upward stroke, rather than hitting the ball down into the opponent's court. Try hitting in the upward swing, just at the apex of the toss and swing — you'll find it works very well.

7. Keep your service toss in front of your body to facilitate a forward motion into the net (attack) position. You will eventually want to do this, so you should begin to adjust to the toss.

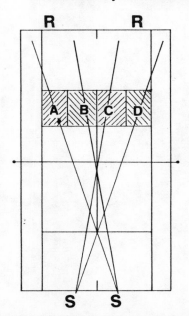

SERVICE TARGET AREAS

Learn to serve into the shaded areas of the court as shown above. As you learn to do this you will: a. Keep the ball deep in the service court. b. Serve to the opponent's forehand (A and C) or to the backhand (B and D).

CHAPTER 9 EVALUATION

1. Which service is considered the basic service for reliability and consistency?

2. Name the three types of service and explain how each differs with reference to stance, grip, ball toss, backswing, contact and follow-through.

3. Which serve is frequently used in doubles?

4. As a second serve, which service is most popular?

5. How would you describe the "backscratch" position used by better players?

6. Describe the body at the instant of contact in the flat service.

7. What is the number one fault of most servers, when common mistakes are made?

8. Where is the follow-through for the topspin (twist) serve?

9. Explain the tossing arm—when is the ball released, what motion is used, where should the trajectory of the ball go?

10. Why should the service toss be made in front of the body, into the court area?

11. There is a definite purpose in keeping the service "deep" in the service court. What are the advantages in doing this?

12. Discuss the comment—"hit up into the service." What does this mean? Why is it important?

122

SERVICE CHECKLIST

NAME _____   P = Poor   F = Fair   G = Good

Divide service courts in half—10 serves to each area.
Check the appropriate box as you observe your partner demonstrate
  his/her ability to serve. Watch several serves to determine
  accuracy in recording your observations.

1. Footwork alighnment is proper at the baseline.   P   F   G
2. Proper grip is used for serve being attempted.   P   F   G
3. Release of ball on toss is at correct arm extension. P   F   G
4. Height of toss is about 1 foot above racket reach.   P   F   G
5. Tosses uses no wrist or elbow motion as lift is made. P   F   G
6. Weight shifts properly into the stroke.   P   F   G
7. Elbow bends fully on racket backswing.   P   F   G
8. Ball is hit at full extension of arm.   P   F   G
9. Slight wrist action is used at contact.   P   F   G
10. Follow-through is across the body.   P   F   G
11. Is the service placement satisfactory?   P   F   G
12. Is there spin on the ball?   P   F   G
13. Is there sufficient speed to keep the receiver
    deep?   P   F   G

Comments: _____
_____
_____
_____

Auxiliary Strokes

In addition to the three basic strokes—forehand, backhand and the service, there are several other types of returns that must be made by the player. Primarily, these are the volley, the smash or overhead, the lob, and the half-volley. As a player becomes proficient in the basic three, the opportunity presents itself to enlarge the depth of the strategy in his/her game. This is done through adequate use of patterns of attack and defense, developed through the execution of these auxiliary strokes. A good player cannot be without them.

THE VOLLEY

The volley is the stroke used to return a ball before it comes into contact with the court. It is usually made from an opponent's drive. It is a relatively simple shot that becomes more complicated as the tempo of the game increases.

Usually a volley is made in the forecourt area—that is, closer to the net and well within the service court. It is an offensive stroke, often winning the point outright. Due to the close position to the net, an angle can be obtained in the volley that frequently prohibits a return by the opponent; thus, its effectiveness as an offensive weapon.

The forehand volley

THE GRIP

Beginners and intermediates will find greater comfort in using the Eastern forehand and backhand grips when hitting a volley. This grip has already been learned, is comfortable, and adapts itself readily to the stroke. Eliminate all wrist action.

The backhand volley

123

BASIC VOLLEY POSITIONS

For high intermediates and advanced players, a service grip—halfway between the Eastern forehand and backhand grip—is preferred. This is primarily due to the increased tempo of the game which prohibits a grip change while at the net. Experimentation and practice will determine which is best for the player according to the style and aggressiveness of that particular individual.

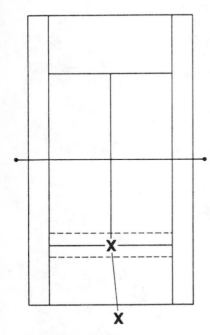

Court Positions for Volley Approach

FOOTWORK

The footwork patterns for the forehand and the backhand volleys are identical—just on opposite sides of the body. In most situations the player will use a basic forward pivot explained earlier. A slight bending of the knees will prove to be helpful as the execution is made.

Since the player is at the net position, there are times when the pace of the ball's approach will not allow proper footwork because of lack of time. In situations like this—and there are many of them—footwork is restricted and concentration on racket position is more important.

BASIC VOLLEY POSITIONS, *continued*

A "check stop" motion of the player will aid greatly in controlling the volley. Simply come to a brief pause just prior to making the intended shot. By pausing, you are able to concentrate on your volley. The "check stop" is used on the approach to the net.

The volley position can be a vulnerable one if the approach shots and volleys are not well executed. Also, the opponent will attempt passing shots to either side that cause additional court coverage for the net player. In situations like this, coverage is made as illustrated in the accompanying diagram.

Cross-over step. This is a step and a pivot of the right foot and a large step across with the left foot, parallel to the net. This is accompanied by a rapid extension of the racket into the path of the ball. This pattern will allow almost all of the court to be covered using a comfortable, basic style of footwork. When used on the backhand side simply reverse the procedure.

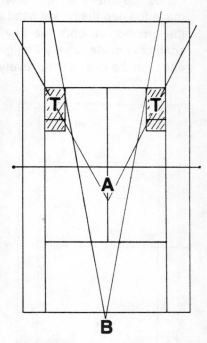

Volley (A) may utilize a wide angle to mount the attack. Compare this with the angle from baseline (B).

STROKE TECHNIQUE

The volley is not a stroke in the context of a forehand or a backhand. It is a stroke that utilizes a blocking motion into the incoming ball. As the ball approaches, hold the racket by the correct grip and move the face of the racket into the path of the ball. A short backswing, about a foot in length is permitted. Contact the ball with a short "punch." Aim the ball downward into the opponent's court, deep, and at a sharp angle. A tight grip is mandatory to stabilize the stroke and to cope with the impact of the incoming ball.

When receiving balls that are above the net, an attempt should be made to punch through the ball at a downward angle. Care must be used to clear the net sufficiently. On volleys made from below the height of the net, the player must exercise caution as the return flight of the ball must be angled upward. This may cause the ball to go out-of-bounds if the hitter is careless. As the ball approaches, the hitter bends the knees to "get down" with the ball. An effort should be made to keep the racket head and hand at the same level, parallel to the ground, on both the low backhand and forehand volley. As contact is made, a very firm grip is maintained, causing the blocking effect on the ball. There is very little follow-through used.

COURT POSITION

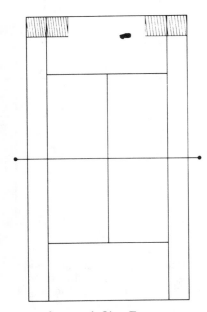

Approach Shot Zones
(Singles and Doubles)

Singles. As the player receives the opportunity to go to the net, he/she returns the short ball away from the opponent. This is usually to an open part of the court and at an angle away from the other player. The direction of the approach shot will determine the position of the net player. The approach shot should have good pace and be deep to the open area of the court. If the receiver is in the home position, place the approach shot deep to the backhand corner, as this is frequently the weakest side, and many players are unable to handle the pressure created by the approaching net rusher.

When receiving a short ball as you go to the net you must use caution in executing the approach shot. This is due to the following reasons: (1) frequently the ball will be below the height of the net; (2) the distance between the point of contact and the opponent's baseline has now become shortened, due to your advancement to the net. Thus, when the total body weight is moved forward in a running pattern it is extremely easy to overhit the ball causing the shot to go out of bounds.

As the approach shot is made, the hitter positions himself/herself about eight feet from the net, on the side in which the ball is hit but close to the midcourt line. This position will allow maximum court coverage for a player. For approach shots that may go down the middle, the only position to obtain is one in the center of the forecourt area.

Doubles. The volley position in doubles is slightly different than that for singles since there are two play- ers covering the court. Each player, being responsible for one side, should be in position halfway be- tween the doubles sideline and the midcourt line. Ideally, both players assume the net position together— the server/receiver joining his or her partner at the net. Coverage of all shots should be complete if both players work harmoniously together. Remember that all shots going down the center should be taken by the player with the forehand return.

Each player should practice con- scientiously so that the point can be won quickly, rather than simply keeping the ball in play. Make your shot crisp and sharp. In doubles, aim at an angle that will win the point outright, particularly down the center between opponents. If this is not practiced, then aim your volley at the feet of the closest net player.

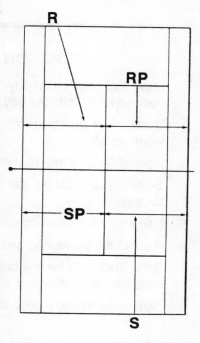

Court Positions for
Volley in Doubles

MOST COMMON VOLLEY ERRORS

Volley goes too long (out of bounds). Tighten your grip and restrict the amount of backswing used to punch the ball. Also, limit the amount of follow-through to increase the length of your ball.

Volley has no speed or crispness. Prepare earlier so you can meet the ball in front of the body for both backhand and forehand. Anticipate well, step into the shot. Watch the ball closely, contacting the ball in the center of the racket face. Punch the ball with a slight downward chop, keep the wrist firm, and contact in front of the body.

Defensive body volleys lacking pace. Use your backhand volley and grip. Move your feet into the ball as it approaches. Contact the ball well out in front. Anticipate early.

TIPS ON TECHNIQUE

1. Move into position quickly. Try to stabilize your footwork before your opponent hits the ball.
2. Select your grip preference early and learn its strengths and weaknesses.
3. If possible, step into your shot.
4. Be sure to contact the ball out in front of the body—forehand and backhand.
5. Use a very firm grip—no wrist action, please!
6. Restrict the backswing and the follow-through. *"Punch the ball."*
7. Bend the knees for low balls, keeping your head and the racket head parallel to the court, if possible.
8. Aim for depth and a good angle.

THE OVERHEAD SMASH

When you are playing the net in the forecourt position and your opponent hits a short high ball easily within reach, you should react by preparing to hit the smash, or overhead, as it is commonly called. The overhead is the most spectacular shot of tennis and is used frequently to win the point outright. Although the shot can be hit from any position on the court, the chances for error become much greater as the player approaches the backcourt area. The closer to the net the better, as the angles are greater and the height of the bounce can be effective, sometimes going over the reach of the racket of the opponent.

The initial movement should be to turn sideways to the net and to the incoming ball. Using the basic side-step motion, move back under the ball, keeping the ball in front of the body at all times. At a point where you anticipate the ball will land, place the weight on both feet, favoring the rear foot primarily. As the stroke is made, shift the weight forward into the stroke, straightening the knees as the reach is extended into the ball. Concentrate on keeping the feet at a 45-degree angle to the net and to the ball, as you shift the body forward. This position will be comfortable, as it closely resembles the serving position.

THE GRIP

The basic grip for the overhead is the Eastern forehand grip. This is primarily due to the familiarity already established with the forehand. Other grips may be used, including the service grip, obtaining a grip

THE SHORT OVERHEAD

THE SCISSOR KICK OVERHEAD
The scissor kick is a method of reaching a ball that is a step away (behind the body). The nature of the "scissor kick" is a balance maneuver to allow immediate recovery combined with a powerful stroke.

halfway between the forehand and the backhand, and the Eastern backhand grip. The latter is used primarily by advanced players. The timing is more critical, however, and the grip causes a closed face on the racket, pulling the ball sharply down into the opponent's court. The grip style will depend largely on the playing skill of the user. As more skill is obtained, the player will move to either the slice grip or the backhand.

FOOTWORK

As in any stroke in tennis, footwork becomes one of the most important ingredients. Proper execution of footwork will move the player into position to play the ball correctly.

In preparing to use the overhead, the footwork begins as soon as the high arc of the incoming ball is recognized. Preparation begins with analyzing where the ball will be hit, and moving your body to this particular area.

THE SCISSOR KICK OVERHEAD, continued

STROKE TECHNIQUE

Basic preparation for most tennis strokes consists of the back-swing, the contact point, and the follow-through. This is also true for the overhead.

Since the original position is at the net, it is assumed that a ready position is maintained. First change the grip. The initial movement is to turn sideways to the net, taking the racket back into the drop-back position behind the back. With the other arm, point toward the incoming ball. This motion is excellent for balance. Continue the racket in the backswing position position, elbow high, racket head dipping well below the back. As the ball approaches the contact point, swing the racket head upward toward the ball. Contact the ball slightly out in front of the body at about "one o'clock." Bring the wrist into the ball very slightly to get the angle down onto the court. An effort should be made to hit *up* and over the ball, rather than "down" on to the ball. The follow-through will be to the opposite side of the

OVERHEAD COURT POSITION

Usually the court position is in the forecourt area. Most overheads are hit from the service courts. Of course, the stroke may be hit from any part of the court, and this is frequently done. However, for best success, the player will achieve more consistency, accuracy and placement by staying relatively close to the net. For very high incoming balls, the wise player will allow the ball to bounce before hitting the overhead. This will provide for better timing in the execution.

Use of the overhead in both singles and doubles will depend entirely on the effectiveness of the offensive and defensive strokes. Strategy will also play a very important part in maneuvering the opponent into positions where the lob will be used, as it is this stroke that causes the overhead to come into play.

OVERHEAD TARGET AREAS

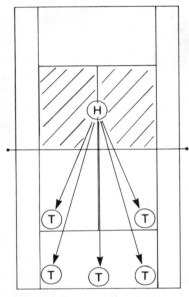

Use angles and/or depth.

TIPS ON TECHNIQUE

1. Keep your eye on the ball at all times and "point the ball in" with the opposite hand.
2. Take the racket back early, behind the back.
3. Don't "get set" too early; keep moving the feet.
4. Stroke smoothly and aggressively.
5. Lead with the racket head; use your wrist.
6. Contact the ball with the arm at a full extension.
7. Follow through with the racket to the left side (diagonally across).
8. Recover quickly in case of a return by your opponent.
9. Practice frequently, using more power as control is established.

MOST COMMON OVERHEAD ERRORS

Ball usually goes long. The ball is hit early and the racket is making contact before the ball passes "one o'clock." The racket face is "open" at contact. Concentrate on hitting with enough wrist to bring the ball down.

Ball goes into the net frequently. Stroke upward into the ball more strongly. Be sure to drop the racket head behind the back before the upward swing.

No power into the ball. Bend the elbow totally, and throw the racket upward into the ball. Utilize the wrist more effectively.

PLAY IT SAFE

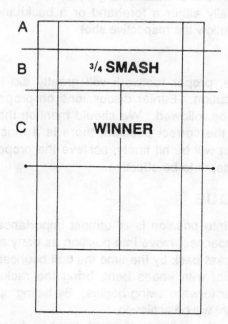

A. Careful here—half speed smash. Keep opponent deep with your return. Let it bounce.

B. Use a three-fourths smash, keeping pressure on the opponent; maintain your position at the net.

C. Go for the winner—everything is in your position at the net.

**How to Play
the Overhead Smash**

THE LOB

If you can picture in your mind the arc of a rainbow, you can visualize the trajectory of the lob. This is probably one of the least used and practiced strokes in tennis. It is not a complicated shot but most players would rather use another stroke when trying to get away from a difficult problem—such as being pressed deep into a corner.

The lob can be either offensive or defensive. However, it is used primarily as a defensive shot. It is rarely practiced to the degree that the technique is mastered. The well-executed lob can be most discomforting to an opponent. The main objectives in lobbing are:

1. To give yourself more time to recover.
2. To push the opponent(s) away from the net.
3. To change pace in your game plan.

THE GRIP

Use either the Eastern forehand or backhand grip, as previously discussed. The lob is actually either a forehand or a backhand groundstroke so the grip will follow the respective shot.

FOOTWORK

As with any groundstroke, proper footwork will greatly aid in determining successful execution. Earlier discussions on proper patterns of footwork should be followed. We should mention that when the player is "set" in the correct position, there is a much stronger chance that the shot will be hit firmly, achieve the proper height, and obtain sufficient depth to be effective.

STROKING TECHNIQUE

As stated earlier, getting into position is of utmost importance. When the incoming ball approaches, move into position as early as possible. Try to have the racket back by the time the ball bounces. From the backswing position, with knees bent, bring the racket slightly under the ball as your forward swing begins. By hitting upward on the shot, lift and height will be achieved.

When you are approaching the contact point with the ball, begin the lift rapidly as though your follow-through is starting now. This will create a high arch on the shot, sufficient to clear the forecourt position occupied by the opponent. By dropping the racket head earlier, more height can be reached, if this is desirable.

The follow-through is most important, as it will serve to guide the ball in the intended direction and height. The follow-through is also used to put spin on the ball.

It should be noted that the normal stroking technique remains the same as a regular forehand or backhand—comfort in the grip and an arm stroke, using the entire arm and racket as one moving extension to *stroke* the ball. Restrict the use of the wrist as much as possible.

TARGET AREA FOR LOBS
(H=Hitter)

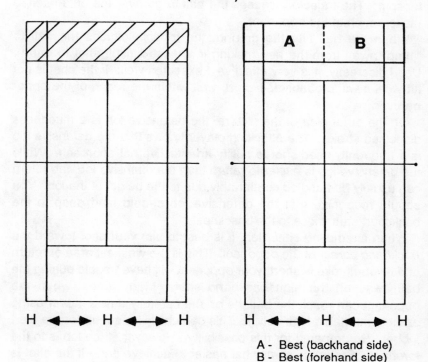

A - Best (backhand side)
B - Best (forehand side)

OFFENSIVE VS DEFENSIVE

Both offensive and defensive lobs are very effective when used properly. The primary differences are found in the direction, disguise, height and spin of the ball. The offensive lob is used as a weapon against an unsuspecting opponent. The stroke can be an outright point winner.

The defensive lob, on the other hand, is usually anticipated by the opponent due to the situation at hand. That is to say, you are being pressed and need more time to recover, so you send a defensive lob up into the air, deep to the backcourt.

By definition, an *offensive lob* is one in which the lob is well disguised with a normal forehand or backhand swing. However, as the racket meets the ball, a lift is provided that creates moderate topspin. The trajectory causes the ball to go over the outstretched racket reach of the opponent.

When the ball hits the ground, the topspin causes the ball to "jump" away from the net, making it a most difficult shot to return. Used discreetly, it is very effective if executed well. If the shot is not hit well, it will probably fall short, well within the reach of the opponent.

On the other side of the picture, the defensive lob is a much less disguised stroke. The attacking player knows that the defensive lob is a frequently used shot to nullify an effective net approach. While the defensive lob is easier to return than the offensive lob, the return can usually be handled comfortably due to the height of the lob. You should recognize that the defensive lob should land deep in the backcourt area, close to the baseline.

When attempting either lob, it is best to aim your shot toward the *backhand corner* of the opponent. This is the weakest area of return and if your stroke is short, your opponent will have trouble putting the ball away on the high backhand shot. Many times, when the opponent can reach the ball, he or she carefully drives it over using an uncomfortable high volley. This can easily be set up for the alert lobber. Be prepared for this possibility. However, if the lob is to the forehand, a return is somewhat easier to achieve and—if the shot is low and within reach—watch out for the overhead that is sure to come. Remember, practice makes a big difference.

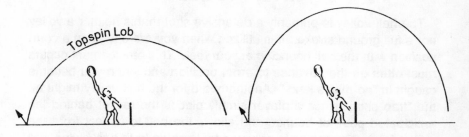

| Offensive lob trajectory (lower) | Defensive lob trajectory (higher) |
| (rarely used) | (frequently used) |

TIPS ON TECHNIQUE

1. Get into position quickly.
2. Use proper footwork.
3. Disguise your intentions if possible.
4. Stroke firmly upward into the ball, using a full follow-through.
5. Keep the racket "on the ball" as long as possible.
6. Recover quickly for the return.

MOST COMMON LOB ERRORS

Lobs are too short. Secure your position earlier. Use the arm more in making the stroke. Drive up and through the ball. Follow through fully. "Carry" the ball on the strings as long as possible.

Ball is mis-hit often. Get ready earlier. Watch the ball more closely. See the ball into the strings of the racket.

Offensive lobs are frequently "put away." Don't "go to the well" too often. Be discreet and use lobs sparingly, preferably from inside the baseline. The deeper you are when you use the lob, the more time the opponent has to reach the ball due to the low trajectory. Topspin lobs are very difficult to execute. Don't use them very much!

HALF-VOLLEY

The half-volley is primarily a defensive shot that is neither a volley nor a full ground stroke. It is utilized when you are caught in a court position with the ball bouncing at your feet. This predicament occurs most often on the advance to a net position and when you become caught in "no man's land." Another word for the half-volley might be the "trap shot," since a player simply places the racket behind the anticipated point of bounce and allows the ball to deflect from the racket face. The stroke is adjusted by keeping both backswing and follow-through to a minimum. Most of the power for the shot is provided by the ball's rebound speed. The point of impact should be slightly in front of your body.

Another analogy that might be used for this shot is the play of a baseball infielder. Oftentimes, infielders will have to "stab with their gloves" at a point where they think the ball will rebound from the playing field. The difference between baseball and tennis is that you have a racket rather than a glove.

The grip for this half-volley should be the same as for the forehand and backhand. Remember to use a "check stop" approach as is required in the volley, keeping the knees bent and the head of the racket nearly parallel to the ground. Also, a short backswing followed by a short follow-through is necessary as you continue to the net position.

The angle at which you hold the racket face will determine the ball's angle of deflection. Of course, the closer you are to the net the more

THE HALF-VOLLEY

you will have to open the face of the racket to raise the ball. A backcourt half-volley will require the face of the racket to be more closed to prevent the ball from rising too high. Remember to have patience since most beginning tennis players will find that mastery of this shot requires considerable practice.

THE DROP SHOT

First and foremost: More points have been lost by hitting drop shots than have been won. It is not a percentage shot. However, there are times in every match when the right shot may be that soft and delicate slice that barely trickles over the net and dies on impact. It can be a devastating weapon, both psychologically and physiologically, when used in an effective manner. Some of the more general principles that govern the drop shot are:

1. Drop shots into the wind are more effective than with the wind.
2. Drop shots in doubles are generally a no-no.
3. The harder the surface, the fewer the drop shots.
4. The best offense against a drop shot is a return drop shot.
5. Drop shots invariably have backspin, thus you must move into the ball more as the ball will not come to you.
6. Do not drop shot from the baseline. Drop only on short balls and then usually at a point across the net which is closest to you.
7. Since most drop shots are hit with a chopping or slice motion, always watch the head of your opponent's racket. When he/she raises the head of the racket higher than the handle, the shot must be a chop shot or drop shot. In any event, you must move forward since the backspin will prevent the ball from bouncing to you.

Drop Shot Trajectory
— heavy backspin

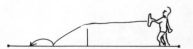

Drop Shot Trajectory
— light backspin

Drop Shot Trajectory
— drop volley at net

CHAPTER 10 EVALUATION

1. Contrast the volley technique as opposed to a regular forehand or backhand stroke.

2. Discuss the pros and cons of the continental grip.

3. What is a "check stop" and how should it be used in volleying?

4. List the two common weaknesses of the volley and techniques to employ for their correction.

5. What is the value of the overhead smash?

6. What would you suggest to the person who generally hits long on the overhead?

7. What about the overhead that constantly goes in the net?

8. Contrast the offensive vs. defensive lob.

9. Define "half-volley" and describe.

10. The direction of your lob is very important with reference to strategy and preventing an effective return by the receiver. What is meant by this?

11. Give several methods of getting to the net to mount the attack against your opponent.

12. How can the player correct volley mis-hits that frequently occur in the stroke?

13. Give several ways to keep the half-volley under control, with a low trajectory over the net.

14. What is the basic grip for the overhead smash? What are the adjustments you would make with a continental grip or a backhand grip? How will the flight of the ball differ?

15. Why is the drop shot a poor risk? Why is seldom successful— and rarely used in doubles?

16. When using a drop shot, why is a hard court such a disadvantage?

Chapter 11

Singles Strategy

THE PERCENTAGE THEORY

"If I can somehow manage to hit one more ball back than you, I'll win this point." This is the philosophy of the tennis player who attempts to pursue the percentage theory. The importance of keeping the ball in play should be paramount in the mind of every player. It is understandable that this is sometimes very hard to do, and cannot be accomplished at all times.

It is a well-known fact that most tennis matches are won on errors. This means that the average and sometimes above-average players tend to defeat themselves by simply making too many mistakes. These players seem content to hit one or two balls back, then impatience gets the best of them and they try to force an opening but don't have the tools with which to do it. Thus, they make an error and this gives the opponent another point.

In good tennis circles, the player who makes the fewest errors or mistakes will usually win. In a match between players A and B, a close analysis would show that if A is the winner, close to 80% of the points won by A are due to common errors by B. This should tell us something. The 20% or so of the points won by A on forcing shots, placements, or aces, are not sufficient to cause much of a problem. Realizing this, we know we must reduce our careless mistakes.

Careless mistakes occur in the entire range of skills that go into the game—from watching the ball, footwork, to stroke technique, and strategy. To be a "pusher," as we call the retriever, is a true compliment.

143

ME

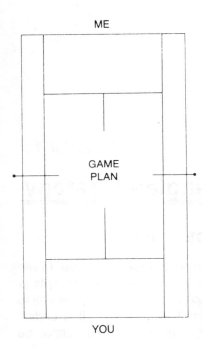

GAME
PLAN

YOU

PLAN YOUR STRATEGY

Most players who find themselves on the opposing side of the net from the pusher know they are in for a long day. They will either have to settle back and play the same game as the pusher—a task they have neither the skill nor patience to achieve, or they must attack and defeat the pusher using placement, power and a forcing type game. Not many players have expertise for these tools either. So after several hours of play, pushers will usually emerge smiling while the opponents stomp off or slink away talking to themselves.

To play percentage tennis, a person must develop an optimum level of conditioning, for this requires a tremendous amount of running to keep the ball in play. A full knowledge of techniques will be necessary, as correct execution will be demanded in the strokes.

A sound knowledge of strategy is also expected since the retriever will find it useful to understand the intent of the opposing player and be able to counter this with correct strokes that work to his purpose.

Remember that this is not an easy undertaking. It requires all the qualities mentioned above, plus great determination. The primary ingredients of percentage tennis are patience and conditioning. Without patience, the percentage theory is not a realistic goal.

Maintaining control by making the fewest errors usually wins a match!

THE DEPTH THEORY

Simply stated, this theory involves the consistent practice of stroking the ball deep into the opponents backcourt. It is very effective to keep your opponent from mounting an attack against you. Imagine being in your home position, two feet behind the baseline. Your opponent strokes a deep ball that lands just inside the line. You have two choices: (2) to back up, giving ground, and play the return from six to eight feet deep; or (2) to play the ball, using a half-volley stroke, from your present position. Your choice will be mandated by your skill level and perhaps the pace of the incoming ball.

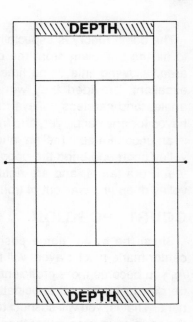

Hit to the shaded areas

An aggressive player wants to begin attacking the opponent at the earliest opportunity, knowing that this additional pressure by *itself* frequently creates a stroking error.

The strategy of the attacker is to wait for a short ball, move in on it, hit an effective approach shot, and secure the net position. By keeping the ball deep, you will accomplish several things:

1. You will keep the opponent away from the net (attack) position.
2. You will allow yourself more time to prepare for each stroke, since the incoming ball is hit from the opponent's backcourt.
3. You will provide yourself added opportunities to go "on the attack," since your opponent's depth in the backcourt will cause many short returns to be hit.
4. Your court position will become more secure, since the possible angles of return will become smaller due to the depth of the hitter.
5. If you hustle, you will realize that from this depth the opponent cannot score an ace on placement against you, simply because he cannot establish the critical angle or speed desired. The shot is hit from too far away and it must travel too far in the air before it reaches your side of the net. The length of the shot provides you with the time needed to make another successful return.

The depth theory is especially pertinent in volleying. You will want to hit the ball away from the opponent, and deep to the backcourt area, allowing little or no time for a return shot. Short angles are excellent, provided they win the point outright. However, short angles and careless volleys that land in the middle of court create havoc for any net player, and frequently cause the loss of the point. It is an uncomfortable feeling, after establishing a position at the net, to volley short and bring the opponent to the attack zone. You begin to feel like a target, and are rightly intimidated. Remember, keep the volley deep and stay out of trouble.

COURT POSITION

Since the basic "home position" is one to three feet behind the center mark, most players will return to this area after hitting the ball. As you become more proficient in your game, part of this success will be due to increased anticipation through observation of the opponent. That is, you will suspect that your opponent will stroke the ball to the open court area rather than directly back to you. This is the same strategy you are also using. Careful observation of the footwork and body position of your opponent will tell you the direction in which the stroke is intended. However, since you cannot be 100% positive of this, you must anticipate all possibilities.

Bisecting the angles of return. When you do this, you are splitting the distance between where the ball can be hit—to your right and left, with you in the center of that angle. This is true on service as well as ground strokes and volleys. Thus, when properly positioned, you will have equal distance to cover on forehand and backhand.

Observe where your opponent stands when receiving service and during play. Frequently he will be standing much to the left of the center of the angle described above. This will probably indicate a weak backhand and an attempt to cover for it.

No-man's land. Generally, tennis play occurs in either the backcourt area or at the net. Beginners and intermediates will stay in the backcourt while advanced players will develop the serve and volley game. The normal drive coming over the net will land within a yard of the service line, in the area commonly referred to as "no-man's land." This area is between the baseline (backcourt) area and the volley (forecourt) position. Young or inexperienced players frequently play in this area, making it their home position. The problem lies with the situation where incoming balls may either land right at your feet or

NO-MAN'S LAND

may go by you as much as head high. This creates anxiety in returning the low shots successfully and in determining if those going past you—still in the air—are going to go out of bounds or are they going to land inside the court. Luck seems to say that those high ones you hit would have gone out, and those you let go always drop inside the baseline. If you play in "no-man's land," pointwise "you get killed." Also, since your position is not close enough to the net to volley the ball effectively and you are not deep enough to allow sufficient time to position yourself properly, you can easily be the recipient of sharp crosscourt strokes or drives that go down the line.

Frequently you must come into the "no-man's land" area to play a short ball. Once you play it, however, you must continue on into the net or return to your baseline. **Do not remain in the center of the court.**

NO-MAN'S LAND

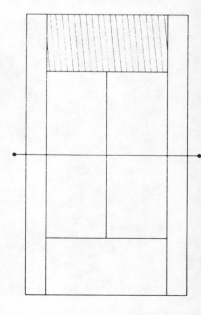

SERVICE STRATEGY

PICKING THE RIGHT SERVE

As we observed earlier, there are three basic serves: the flat serve, the slice serve and the twist or topspin. Every advanced player should develop the ability to execute each serve properly. Often one type of service is more effective than another against an opponent. You will benefit greatly if you can discover which type of serve gives your opponent the most trouble and then use this serve to maximum benefit.

On the right side of the baseline, the server will usually stand from one to three feet from the center mark. This position will be maintained no matter which serve is used. This angle will promote service to the opponent's backhand and will allow for proper court coverage on service returns. It is permissible to stand as far to the right as the singles sideline, although this is rarely done due to the amount of court area left open on the backhand side.

When serving from the left side of the baseline, the server's position is about three to five feet from the center mark. Most players will stand a little farther away from the center mark on this side due to: (1) a desire to get a sharper angle toward the opponent's backhand and (2) a feeling of more security toward the forehand side for returned serves.

Generally the keynote to serving is variety. You will find a significant advantage in hitting different types of serves to your opponent. You should determine very early in a match which serve seems to give your opponent the most difficulty and use this serve most of the time. Hit about 85% of your serves to the

Service Courts: Right Service Court (Top); Left Service Court (Bottom)

backhand of the receiver, as this in itself will usually create many errors in service returns. Also many returns from poor backhands will be so weak that they can easily be attacked.

Vary the type of service used. If your favorite serve is a slice service to the backhand, occasionally use a topspin or flat serve just to change the pace. This will often throw the opponent off insofar as timing and positioning are concerned, thus creating an error. Move your opponent around as you serve. Place most serves to the backhand, some to the forehand, and some directly into the body. The slice service toward the backhand that curves into the body is extremely effective when used discreetly.

Frequently the first and second serve vary greatly. Many inexperienced players serve very hard, inaccurate balls on the first effort, then follow by a very slow-paced ball that, while secure from a double fault, does not do anything other than to put the point in play. This type of serve can easily be handled by the receiver, who usually puts the server on the defensive by hitting a solid, well-placed return.

Logic will show that a better procedure to follow will be to have two serves of about the same speed, but with different types of spin; for example, a flat first serve followed b a slice or a topspin serve. Another combination is to use a slice service

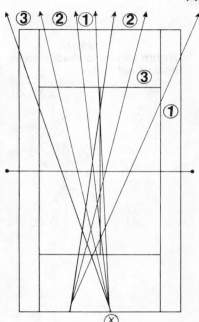

Placement of service
Forehand and backhand courts

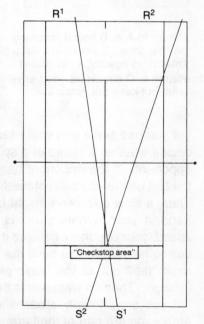

SERVICE APPROACH CHECK
Server should pause at the checkstop area when following serve to the net. Read the service return, then continue.

Return service to shaded areas against net rusher.

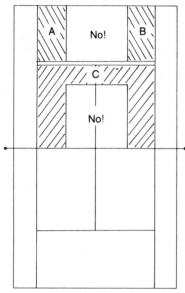

1. Return to A or B only if receiving on that side. Don't return deep crosscourt against a net rusher.
2. Return to C should be good anytime, but keep the return *low*.

as a first serve, followed by a twist (topspin) serve. The use of spin—either slice or topspin—gives more clearance to the ball as it goes over the net. As a result, it is more secure against the double fault.

Remember these basic points: **(1) Placement**—getting the ball deep to the opponent's backhand, right at the opponent or to the forehand corner; **(2) Speed**—sufficient speed to keep the opponent in the backcourt area when returning your serve; and **(3) Spin**—enough to allow the ball to clear the net, then to take the ball down on the court, and enough spin to curve the ball in the desired direction (slice) or to kick up a higher bounce on contact with the court (twist).

At times, variety or change is necessary. Although you have a good serve, if you constantly serve to the same spot again and again, your opponent will adjust and begin returning more effectively against you. So keep your opponent guessing.

If you use serve and volley tactics as your basic strategy, you must decide whether a speed or a spin serve is most effective against your opponent. If the opponent handles your speed well, he may return the ball before you can establish your position for the approach volley. Thus, a slow spin serve might be more advantageous. On the other hand, if your favorite serve is a spin serve but due to the slower speed, your opponent handles it easily and causes you to make errors due to his return, you have the other problem. There are things you must "feel" out as you begin playing the match. Think the problem through. Then do whatever is best in the given situation.

If you are primarily a baseline player—you stay in the backcourt area—you are part of the large majority of tennis players. The baseline player uses the service as a means of starting the point. Granted, the serve is hit as hard as control will allow (sometimes harder!). On occasion, this will win the point by itself. However, most of the time the player will use his/her ground strokes to win the point, coming to the net only as a matter of necessity when a very short ball is received. Beginning and intermediate tennis is played with this strategy in mind.

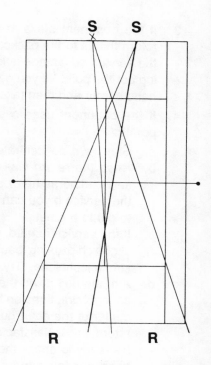

STRATEGY WHEN RECEIVING SERVICE

As your opponent prepares to serve to you, you will probably have many things going through your mind. "Where should I stand?" "What type of serve will be used?" "Will the server come to the net? "How fast will the serve be hit?"

Bisecting angles of return (service)

If you worry slightly about these things, welcome to the vast majority of serious tennis players. Many leading tennis professionals agree that the service is the most important stroke in tennis. If this is true, and we have no reason to doubt it, then the service return must be equally as important from the receiver's point of view.

We know that in good tennis if you can win the games you serve and break the opponent's serve one time, you will win the set. Thus, being able to return serve effectively is extremely important. Here are the key points in returning service:

1. *Place the ball in play.* Try not to make an error on the return. This is the most important factor in receiving service. Give the opponent a chance to make an error. **Return the ball.**
2. Maintain a court position according to the opponent's serve. Remember to bisect the angle of return, allowing equal coverage to the forehand and the backhand. (See illustration.)

3. If the opponent stays at the baseline, try for a medium speed return that is to the backcourt area. If you can do this effectively, the service advantage is lost. Now you can concentrate on playing out the point. If you get a short return, drive deep to the backhand corner and then take the net position.

4. If the opponent uses a serve and volley strategy follow these points:
   a. *Stay calm,* concentrate, anticipate the serve.
   b. *Keep the return low*—usually to the feet of the server at the service line as he or she comes toward the net. Move in on the service if you can to cut down on the time the server has to get to the net.
   c. If the service is hard, with spin, just try to *block it* back with a slight chip using backspin. Disregard using a full groundstroke technique. Try for a low return.
   d. Aim the ball down the sideline. This will cause the server to change directions on the approach. However, if you go to the center of the court due to lack of time for preparation of your return, this is satisfactory.
   e. Be ready to attack the opponent's approach shot. If you hit a good service return, you can capitalize on your next shot. Use lobs and drives effectively now.
   f. Occasionally use the lob to throw the opponent off guard. Lob toward the backhand side.
   g. Be consistent; don't make careless errors. Give your opponents the opportunity to beat themselves Patience is required.

TYPES OF GAMES

A tennis player's skill will determine the styles of play that may be used effectively. These are determined primarily by the competency established in practice patterns using the strokes of the game.

1. 3-Stroke Game—uses the service, forehand, and backhand only. This is played as a baseline game, whether singles or doubles.
2. 5-Stroke Game—uses the three strokes mentioned above plus the volley and the smash. This is a more aggressive style of play frequently found in intermediate tennis.

3. All-Court Game—uses all of the strokes mentioned above plus the auxiliary shots including the offensive and defensive lobs, half-volley, chop and drop shots, lob volley and the drop volley. There are not many intermediate players who have a good command of all these strokes, and probably very few advanced players. This skill level is primarily found in higher levels of competitive play. Even then, many of these shots are not used effectively.

Remember, no matter what your style of play, there is always plenty of room for improvement.

BASIC POINTS OF SINGLES STRATEGY

1. Keep the ball in play. Give your opponent another chance to make an error.
2. When possible, keep the play to the opponent's backhand, as this is usually the weaker of the two ground strokes.
3. Look for openings in your service attack—*move* the receiver. If you notice the receiver moving to cover your service to the backhand with a forehand return (done as you toss the ball) then plan to occasionally direct your serve to the forehand corner. Aim your serve into the receiver's body once in a while to keep him/her guessing.
4. Mount the attack on any short ball you receive. Remember, by coming to the net and driving to the opponent's backhand on the approach, you are forcing the opponent to (1) worry about your attack, (2) hit a winner, (3) force an error on your part, (4) lob (most likely up to the advanced level).
5. Keep in mind that your success in establishing control of the net is based on *what* you did to get there—your approach shot, its accuracy and depth.
6. Occasional play to the forehand of your opponent will tend to open up opportunities for attacking the backhand area. Be sure to keep your opponent deep.
7. Use the strokes in your game that will give you the highest percentage of success in the situation at hand.
8. Be very careful about using drop shots, drop volleys, sharp angle volleys, etc. They have a low percentage of success and often cause much trouble to the hitter.
9. Utilize a "check stop" on your way to the net as it greatly facilitates movement laterally to play the incoming ball.

10. When playing against a net rusher, use the stroke that you have the most confidence in and the one that has the greatest percentage for success.
11. Try to place your return at the feet of the net rusher, thus causing an upward volley on the ball to clear the net. This, in turn, should make you alert to the short return, allowing you the chance to move in for the kill.

QUESTIONS AND ANSWERS ABOUT PLAYING

After hitting a very good lob I have a tendency to rest on my heels behind my baseline. Is this bad? Well, it's not good. When you hit a great lob over your opponent at the net, you have put your opponent in a defensive position. Thus, you should close, forcing the opponent into a lower percentage shot.

I like to follow my serve to the net but do not seem to be getting in far enough for my first check stop and volley. Any advice? Several things could be causing this. First of all, you could just be slow. However, you might be throwing your toss either too far behind you (for topspin) or too far to the right so that your first step is not straight in toward the net.

I seem to constantly get caught by a quick lob over my head. What should I do? You may be closing too tightly on the net. Also, you should know who the good lobbers are and as soon as you see a lob situation and/or motion, then back pedal a few steps for protection. It is always easier to close back in than retreat if the opponent hits a short shot.

I have an opponent who destroys me with his serve and volley game. What can I do against him? It could be he is just a better player; however, you might try the following:
1. Determine whether you are losing the points by missing the return of serve or whether your opponent is winning the points with his volley. If you are missing the service return, ease off but make up your mind ahead of time where you are going to return the ball. If the serve is on your backhand, go down the line; if it is on your forehand, go crosscourt. The important thing is to put the ball in play.

2. If, on the other hand, you have been chipping the ball at your opponent's feet and he is still putting the volley away, try hitting out a little more.
3. If the opponent has a weak second serve, run around it for a forehand.
4. Moving back will give you more time but, of course, this allows your opponent to close more tightly. Moving in tight against the less powerful serve often forces mistakes.
5. Make your opponent change his volley pattern. For example, if he is going crosscourt for safe valleys, then move early in that direction, forcing him to change the shot.

I am not able to play more than once or twice a week. What one or two tips would help me most? Most pros agree that getting the racket back early and physical conditioning are probably the two most important tips for a weekend player.

I have noticed some of the pros wearing rings and watches while playing. What do you think about the practice? The pros generally wear these objects because they are endorsements and they are being paid to do so. Anything that is distracting or interferes with your "touch" or "feel" of the racket will hamper your performance.

My opponent made a great shot but I was able to get to it a split second before it bounced twice and then hit a winning placement. My opponent claimed the ball bounced twice. However, I was sure I had made the shot in time and refused to give up the point. Was I legally correct in doing so? Yes, see paragraph 33.1 of the Rules.

My first serve is erratic and seldom goes in but my second serve is very reliable. Why is this? Probably this is due to your hitting the first serve too hard. Check the fundamentals—take your time, concentrate, and slow the serve down. Remember to keep the toss in front of your body and high enough to really reach for it. It will work; give it time and lots of practice.

156

Every time I hit a return back that lands short, my opponent comes to the net. This really bothers me. What can I do to eliminate this problem? Very simply, raise your stroke trajectory and hit the ball deeper in the opponent's court. Remember, you gave the opponent the opportunity to come to the net when you hit short; he had to come in to get your shot!

What can I do to win more points? I seem to beat myself most of the time. Understand the meaning of percentage tennis; then realize the importance in getting *each and every* ball back over the net. Anticipate early, set up quickly and aim for the backcourt area. Give yourself good net clearance. Practice this procedure frequently. You should improve dramatically!

My opponent has a hard serve. I find I am usually late in my swing trying to return it. What can I do to improve my return percentage? Your problem is a lack of time to accomplish a full swing in your return. Try blocking the ball back with a little underspin used for accuracy. You should see good results quickly.

I am getting killed trying to return my opponent's service. Are there any tips that might help me determine whether he is going to hit flat, topspin, or slice? Most tennis players do not study their opponents enough. Your first clue will be the toss and the grip the opponent uses. A toss out to the side probably indicates a slice; a toss to the left and behind the head means topspin; and a toss straight up usually means a hard and flat serve. Remember also that the more your opponent shifts his hand from an Eastern grip to the backhand, the more spin you will be looking at. Returning a very fast serve requires a fast turn-hit motion. This means the racket must be cocked as you turn so the result is a step-hit motion much like a one-two punch. One way to speed up the process is to first determine the direction of the ball by the toss, then take a very slight hop in that direction to get your weight flowing forward and on the balls of your feet. From there on it depends on your skill level.

I have heard that playing tennis Is a good way to burn calories. How good Is It? You have heard right. However, the number of calories you burn is related to how many pounds you are pushing around on the court and how much distance you travel. On the average, a woman will expend 400 calories per hour playing singles, while a man will burn about 600. Doubles play will reduce expenditures for both men and women to about two-thirds of this number.

Is there anything new on the best fluid replacement? From what we can determine, water remains the number one choice. However, if you stomach can handle it, you might try a mixture of tomato juice and water. Both absorb quickly and the tomato juice has some potassium and sodium which will help replace that lost.

As a serve and volley player, what can I do for an edge against the hard-hitting two hander? (1) Since most two-handers hit topspin returns and topspin players prefer to hit higher balls, slice the serve a lot and keep it low. (2) Most two handers like to "groove" on a serve so it is critical that you never give away location or type of serve. In short, you must keep them guessing. (3) Since the two-hander likes to hit at the high point of the bounce, this affords you more time to close in on the net. It is important that you close as tightly as possible.

What is the one best piece of advice for a beginning tennis player? To set realistic goals according to your aspirations. This means that if you want to be a tournament player, your training program will be at a different level than if your goal is to be a good club player who plays for self-enjoyment and exercise.

What one tip could you give me to play better on clay? It has been said that clay and other soft surfaces favor the thinking player. So since you are not going to blow anyone off a clay court, sit back and be prepared to play long points by maintaining concentration and setting up your shots in a series.

I play pretty well in most matches, but when the match goes into a tie breaker, I can't seem to win. Any advice? The thing you must remember is that every point is a key point. In a regular game you can get fancy once in a while or go for the big one and if it doesn't work, you can still retrench and possibly win. The tie breaker simply does not allow much room to recover once you fall behind. Play the tie breaker exactly as you played to get there. Remember to hit your high percentage shots and, above all, "hang in there." You will be amazed at how many of your opponents will fold if you just keep "hanging in."

As a recreational or club player, why should I learn to hit topspin? The main reason is control plus speed. Topspin allows you to hit the ball harder because the spin on the ball causes it to drop rapidly after crossing the net.

I do pretty well playing against one-handed players but seem to have a terrible time against two-handers. Any advice? There are several things you might try doing. For instance:
- Try hitting straight at a two-hander. This prevents the free-swinging two-hander from getting that big, looping swing.
- Try short shots into the midcourt area. Two-handers usually prefer a baseline game and either they must do a lot of running up and back or you may put them in less familiar territory.
- Hit low slicing shots. The low bouncing shot prevents the two-hander from effectively stiffening the left hand to generate power.
- Hit passing shots low and to the backhand. The low two-hand backhand volley forces your opponent to turn his wrist into and unnatural position.
- Aim for the T zone—where the singles sidelines meet the service line. Low wide shots are tough for two-handers.
- Don't worry about too many different kinds of shots from two-handers—only topspin and lots of it.

CHAPTER 11 EVALUATION

1. Most tennis matches are lost, rather than won. Explain.

2. When two players meet on the court, the winner will usually have a large percentage of points "given" to him/her by the loser. What percentage of points would this total?

3. List several items a player should concentrate on to correct a poor percentage of returns.

4. What should the philosophy be of the player who expounds on the percentage theory in tennis?

5. Explain the depth theory. How can it assist you in becoming a better player? List several strategy points associated with the depth theory.

6. What is meant by bisecting the angle of return?

7. How can you utilize the serve as an effective weapon against your opponent? List several strategy points that will mean easy points for you if you follow them.

8. If the server does not come to the net following the service, what should you attempt on the return? If the server comes in, what should you do?

9. As receiver of the service your first thought should be to do what?

10. Define the following:

    a. 3-stroke game

    b. 5-stroke game

    c. All-court game

11. What strategy will you use against a net rusher? Explain the reasoning behind the selection of shots you would make.

12. Why is it desirable to lob to the backhand side of a net rusher?

13. Generally, how does a "baseliner" win? What talents must the player possess to be secure in this type of game?

14. Describe the sequence of "working" a point as you might move from the baseline rally to the net.

The Doubles Game

PICKING YOUR DOUBLES PARTNER

One of the nice things about playing doubles in tennis is the opportunity afforded to make many new friendships. If, however, you are interested in playing serious long-term doubles, it might be wise to give some thought in picking your doubles partner. Some of the factors worthy of consideration are:

1. Personality of partners.
2. The type of game each plays—i.e., baseline or serve.
3. Handedness of the partner. Ideally a right-hander and a left-hander should make the strongest combination since each has forehand crosscourt return of service.
4. In most cases, the strongest backhand should play the left court.

DOUBLES STRATEGY

The game of doubles is a team sport. Granted, there are only two members on the team, but when play begins you are very much supportive of each other, as players would be in any sport. There are several ways that singles and doubles differ.

1. The court is nine feet wider in doubles, bringing the alleys into use.
2. Both players share equal responsibility in covering court space.
3. General strategy involves both players going into the "attack" (net) position as quickly as possible and playing side by side.
4. You must depend upon your partner to adequately keep *you* out of trouble with his strokes.
5. Groundstrokes become less important in doubles. The serve, volley, and overhead are the strokes most often used.
6. Placement of shots is more critical in doubles since an effort must be made to keep the ball away from the player(s) at the net.
7. Doubles is a much faster game, with drives being cut off by net volleys and sharp angles being hit.

A broader variety of strokes is utilized in doubles. This requires that doubles players practice all shots frequently so that when called upon to use them, they will be readily available.

Three types of doubles games are played today. They are basic doubles, Australian doubles, and "club" or recreational doubles. These three vary in technique, court positions, and strategy.

BASIC DOUBLES

Court positions for basic doubles place the players in the location where they will be able to capitalize most effectively on shots that come their way. The positions are advantageous for partners and options are open depending on the strategy they wish to use.

PARALLEL THEORY

The parallel theory is a theory whereby doubles partners play parallel to each other. They are responsible for covering all action in their respective halves of the court. Thus, their area of responsibility is from the center service line to the doubles sideline, on their side from the baseline to the net. Often players feel they are responsible for "all the net" or "all the baseline." This would dictate an up and back position and would leave too much area open. In good doubles play, both players are "up and back" frequently, but always they play parallel to each other.

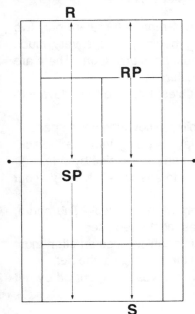

In the diagram we see the basic positions for doubles. The server (S) stands about three feet to the right of the center mark. The partner of the server (SP) stands in the left service court, about four feet from the singles sideline and about six to eight feet from the net. The receiver (R) stands at the baseline awaiting the service. R should bisect the angle of the service. The receiver's partner (RP) stands on the service line. These basic positions are used to begin each point. From here the initial strategy begins and will depend on the knowledge and stroke production of the players involved.

As the service is made, the server moves up into the court, trying to get as close to the net as possible before the receiver returns the ball. Usually a step inside the service line is all that can be achieved, but this depends upon the service and the speed of the server. As the service return passes over the net, the server uses a half-volley or a volley and progresses on in to establish a true net position. At this point, the server is alongside his/her partner, generally parallel to the net. Usually the receiver (R) will also move toward the net after the service is returned. The receiver's partner (RP) is stepping toward the net in an effort to cut off the volley. Thus, we are frequently confronted with all 4 players at the net, looking for an opening to force an error or to hit a winner.

AUSTRALIAN DOUBLES

This method of play changes the formation most generally used in doubles play. The RP is located as explained under parallel theory. The SP now places himself/herself in the service court in front of the *receiving net player*. The server, upon delivering the service, must now assume total responsibility for the returns coming "down the line" rather than crosscourt. The Aussie innovation will disturb those players accustomed to standard formations but will not make a difference to good players. See diagrams for court positions used in Australian doubles.

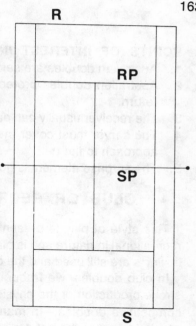

Forehand Court

AUSTRALIAN DOUBLES

Backhand Court

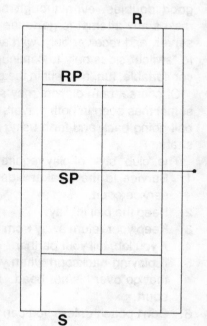

164

POINTS OF INTEREST IN AUSTRALIAN DOUBLES
1. Australian doubles are seldom used in good competition.
2. Australian doubles protect against a sharp crosscourt service return.
3. The receiver usually can easily return down the line.
4. The server must cover the alley frequently, thus eliminating the approach to the net.
5. The surprise element is good on occasion, if not overused.

CLUB OR RECREATIONAL DOUBLES

This style of play is presently worldwide in scope. It is primarily recreational in nature and is played for fun. However, the competitive instincts are still used and the desire to win is sometimes intense.

In club doubles, we frequently find players who do not have the stroke production or the physical prowess to play aggressive "basic" competitive doubles. In many instances, the footwork and hustle needed to get to the net are just not a part of the player. Also, trying to follow a somewhat weak serve to the net would be foolish.

Thus we find that many players tend to play a formation of one-up, one-back. While this does not resemble two players in the center of the court in an "I" formation, it does have the basic characteristics of good doubles, even though neither the server nor the receiver makes any attempt to go to the net. Play is frequently between the server and receiver only, with an occasional lob causing the players to "switch" sides only to continue this basic style. It is very popular, comfortable, fun, and within the general capabilities of most players.

Of course, both players may stand anywhere on the court. This is sometimes seen in both players staying on the baseline, keeping the ball going back and forth using crosscourt drives and down the line shots.

The "club" style of play requires certain basic responsibilities:
1. Service to the weaker side of an opponent and deep into the service court.
2. Keep the ball in play.
3. Keep your return away from the net player.
4. If you lob, tell your partner.
5. If playing backcourt when your partner is at the net, cover lobs that go over his/her head. In other words, "switch" sides of the court.
6. Don't poach unless you can win the point.

Doubles is a lifetime sport. The four players in this photo have 283 years of combined playing time.

By playing together frequently, teammates can easily complement each other, developing consistent placements, strategic volleys and accurate lobs. Then the team becomes hard to defeat.

TENNIS STRATEGY FOR DOUBLES

Good doubles is based upon the server's being able to hold serve; that is, to win the game you are serving. To do this requires proper placement, spin and speed on the serve. Remember, it only takes one service break to win or lose a set.

Doubles strategy demands that the best server on your team should serve first. This is because you will have an easier time holding service with your stronger server. The server should consider the following points when serving:

1. Determine which side (forehand or backhand) your opponent has the most difficulty with in returning serve, then attack that side. This is generally the backhand side!

2. Which serve gives the receiver more trouble? Slice, twist, flat? Go for that one frequently.

3. Look for an opening in the position of the receiver. This will create a weak return.

4. Keep enough speed on your serve to keep the receiver deep and protect your partner at the net.

5. Aim at the corners frequently to force a weak return.

6. Come to the net as often as you can.

"I am poaching."   "I am staying."

7. Use variety in your serve. Don't allow the opponent to anticipate your serve with regularity. Mix them up.

8. Take your time on your serve.

9. Get your first serve in. It gives your team a great psychological advantage and your opponent will be deeper in his backcourt than on the second serve.

10. Use lots of spin on your second serve, but keep the opponent deep.

11. Let your partner know that he should try for any ball within his reach. Do poach, whenever feasible.

12. Determine which player is the weaker, and play most of your shots to this opponent.

13. Arrange hand signals with your net man so you will know what he plans to do. Example—to poach or to stay? See the photos.

14. Increased spin will allow more time to take the net.

15. A left-hander usually serves on the sunny side.

16. Angle is almost as important as speed since it can pull the receiver wide and open the middle.

17. Never follow a weak serve to the net.

18. Get to the net as quickly and as often as you can. The team at the net has a 90% chance of winning the point.

19. When both opponents are at the net, keep your shots down the middle and low. This often creates confusion as to "who plays the ball" and results in an error.
20. The three formations for doubles play are:
    Both at the net: advanced, high intermediate
    Both at the baseline: beginner, intermediate
    One up, one back: beginner, intermediate
21. Remember to protect your partner at the net. Good stroke execution will allow this. Follow these guidelines:
    a. Get your *first serve in.* Serve *deep* to the opponent's backhand.
    b. Return deep to the crosscourt corner if the server doesn't come to the net. Attack the net with your partner immediately.
    c. Return the serve to the feet of the advancing server.
    d. Volley low so opponents must hit up on the ball.
    e. Lob deep over the head of the opposing net player.
    f. Drive down the alley if the opponent poaches early.

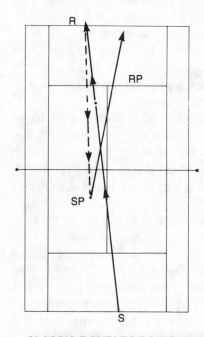

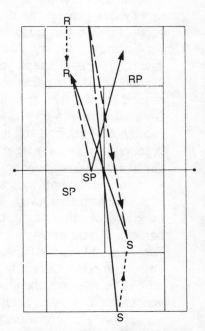

CLASSIC DOUBLES POINT #1
R serves to R
R returns to SP
SP wins point with volley

CLASSIC DOUBLES POINT #2
S serves to R
R returns to S (moving in)
S returns to R (moving in)
R returns to SP (poaching)
SP volleys for a winner.

STRATEGY WHEN RECEIVING

Receiving serve is just as important as serving. If you have a good return of service you can break the opponents' serve and win a game. This takes a lot of practice and should become one of your most sound strokes.

As in serving, returning the serve should be done with planning, care and deception. Using variety is important, but not to the point that careless errors become rampant in your game. Follow these guidelines as you think about your service returns:

1. **Placing the ball in play.** It is absolutely imperative that the ball is placed in play each time your opponent serves. If nothing else, simply hack it back without trying to put special placement or spin on the ball. Do not defeat yourself. At least make your opponent do it.

2. **Position for a return of service.** Always bisect the angle between you and the server. That is, draw an imaginary line through the service area splitting the angle in an equal manner. In some cases, you may be able to cheat on your opponent by slightly overplaying the backhand. Certainly, the opponent's serve should be tested to see if this can be done.

3. **Be bouncy. Worry your opponent.** Being bouncy does several things—it keeps you light on your feet and it distracts the server. This is particularly true if you walk up on the server's second serve just as he or she is about to hit.

4. **Defensing the serve and volley.** Sometimes a chop or slice shot hit low and soft to the opponent's feet is very effective in countering the net rusher who likes to volley. If the ball is kept low at least your opponent cannot put it away but will have to volley up on the ball, thus allowing you an excellent opportunity to put the next shot away.

5. **In general, do not lob a return of serve.** This is particularly true in singles. There are several reasons for this. First of all, it is very difficult to lob a serve that has an excessive amount of spin. Secondly, a lob must be a nearly perfect shot for it to be effective and there is too much margin for error if this is not achieved. Also, even if it is a perfect lob, the opponent will usually have an opportunity to return the ball. Thus, even if a perfect shot is made, you do not have a clear winner.

6. If the server has an extremely fast serve and you are playing on a hard surface, it is probably better to return service one or two

steps behind the baseline. With most tennis players, it is generally a good idea to return the first serve from near the baseline and to move in one or two steps for the second serve.

7. If your opponent is consistently winning his/her serve, change your procedures. That is, whatever you are doing, do something different.

8. **Playing percentages.** Always use your percentage return. That is, hit the shot which will most often place the ball in play.

9. When returning serve, always try to return it as deep as possible. The best place is one to two feet inside the baseline, preferably at the opponents' weak side.

10. If the opponent is consistently scoring on his/her serve, change the target. That is, move in very close, overplay on one side or the other, but **change the target** so your opponent is not looking at the same target each time.

11. Some people grow accustomed to having an opponent play on or near the baseline. Thus when the opponent moves in extremely close, they will usually try to put more spin or speed on the ball and frequently lose their effectiveness on the first serve.

12. **Always remember that tennis is a game of percentage.** Close only counts in horseshoes. To be a winner, you must hit those shots which give you your best percentage and not hit those shots which are less productive.

13. If you are most effective from the baseline, then you should not take the net unless forced to do so. Conversely, if your opponent dos not lob well and you have the good volley then, by all means, attack at every opportunity.

14. If an opponent gives even the slightest indication that he/she dislikes one of your shots (for example, a drop shot, since some players are very lazy), then by all means, keep chipping away.

15. In general, return a drop shot with your own drop shot, since most persons who hit the drop shot retreat to the baseline.

16. Most shots that are missed as a player rushes the net are hit long because the average player does not compensate for his/her forward body momentum.

Remember that your partner is moving up on your service return. If you are missing shots, check your fundamentals: footwork, eye on the ball, turning the side, and good stroke production. Stay with basic tennis strategy. Rarely vary from it.

USE OF THE VOLLEY, SMASH AND LOB

In doubles the basic strategy of the game emphasizes the importance of net play. The initial alignment of players, both in serving and receiving, indicates a strong emphasis toward establishing an attack position at the net—thus, the volley, the smash and the lob become most important. If you are attempting to get to the net, the volley and/or the lob will assist you. Also, once there, the overhead smash will help you.

Let's briefly review the use of these three strokes as they pertain to basic doubles strategy.

The Volley. Remember this stroke is used as an offensive weapon, attempting to win the point by an angle or to force a weak return. On the serving side, the server's partner is already established at the net hoping to cut off a drive and win the point. The server will serve and come to the net, often using the volley to get there.

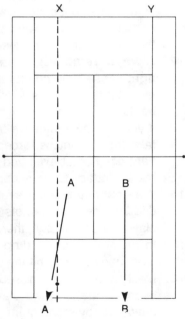

Once at the net, the volley will be used to assist in winning the point. The receiving team is also positioned to take the net position if the serving team doesn't beat them to it! The receiver's partner is at the service line ready to come in and the receiver, if the server doesn't come in, should return deep and approach the net. The volley is the basic point winner in good doubles, as both players are at the net.

The Smash. Of course, you had rather use the smash than the volley because you will win the point quicker and more often. However, to use a smash one needs to have an opponent send a lob that is short enough for smash execution. This can usually be done by a forcing ground stroke, service, or volley. Since everyone will be playing at the net, all doubles participants should have a good overhead.

COVERING THE LOB

Using the Parallel Theory of Coverage Each player covers all shots (lobs included) on his or her side. In this illustration, X lobs deep behind A, who easily retreats and covers the return.

The Lob. This is the most under-used shot in tennis. However, if executed properly, it can be devastating to any tennis player. In doubles, you know that the opponents will be attacking the net position; this makes them vulnerable to the lob. Proper use of the lob will cause them to be pushed back from the attack position to a defensive position at the baseline. Also, if your lob is to their backhand and has some topspin, you can easily attack behind this shot. So practice lobbing and enjoy the problems you give your opponents.

As seen in this chapter, doubles is a great game. Unlike singles, teamwork is involved. Good players complement each other. However, partners must know basic strategy and have good execution of fundamentals. You must understand what is expected of you insofar as serving, receiving, net play, court coverage and teamwork. Once you really "get into the game," you'll find great enjoyment in this new-found challenge.

CANADIAN DOUBLES

A unique system of play called "Canadian Doubles" is sometimes found at recreation areas and clubs. This game simply uses three players instead of the normal number of four for doubles play. Canadian doubles is not an official game and should be used for fun and recreation only.

When using Canadian doubles, the singles person is playing two

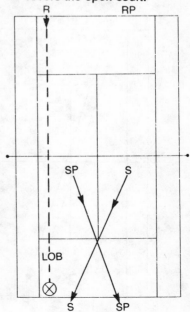

COVERING THE LOB
Server covers the lob.
SP covers open area.
R and RP move to the net.

COVERING THE LOB
S and SP both at the net.
S takes the lob and SP
covers the open court.

172

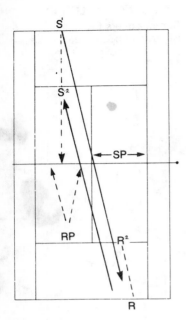

Court positions of advanced players and net positions after serving and receiving. Both are on the attack and try to achieve the net position. Volley and half-volley are usually used.

Left: Comparison for "club" doubles using the one up and one back system. Play is directed S to R to S and so forth. S and R cover all deep shots to either side, with no poaching by either SP or RP. R and S maintain positions at baseline; RP and SP maintain forward positions. **Right:** Positions for beginner doubles. Both players maintain positions at the baseline on each side. Each player is responsible for his/her half of the court, and rarely advances to the net. Most points are won here on errors rather than placements.

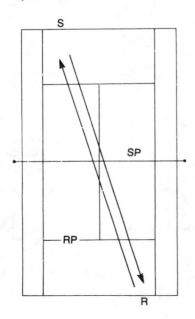

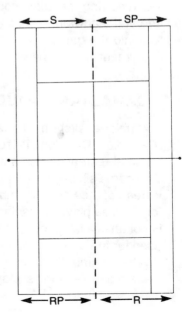

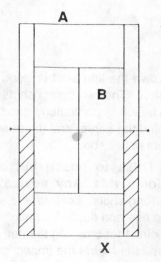

opponents. The singles player must cover his/her singles court only, while the two opponents must cover their doubles court. Rules of tennis are followed for the singles and doubles players with regard to their court area of coverage.

Since this is not a recognized system of singles or doubles, *fun* is the main attraction. The game is merely a substitute for being short one player.

A and B must cover the entire doubles court; X must over only the singles court (the alleys are not used).

QUESTIONS AND ANSWERS ABOUT DOUBLES

I once played a pretty good singles game, but now that I am getting older and do not play as much I have switched to doubles. How can I improve my doubles game quickly? There is no such thing as quick success in tennis; however, if you will concentrate on the following your doubles game will improve:

1. Keep the ball lower when hitting from the baseline, and when in trouble, aim for the net strap.

2. Take the serve sooner. This means moving in or up to return first and second serves.

3. Improve your serve, return of serve, volley and lob.

4. Know your partner and communicate.

My partner does not play as well as I. Should he play the backhand or forehand court? Since the important points are most often played in the backhand court, generally the best player should be in that position. Also, this usually places the strongest forehand guarding the middle and places the strongest overhead in a high percentage position.

I play a lot of doubles and am continually harassed and intimidated by anyone who "poaches" on me. What should I do? An aggressive poacher can frequently win more points by causing opponent errors than by actually putting the ball away. The first thing you must do is keep him anchored and that can best be achieved by giving him a sharp shot to the body. A down-the-line shot is good but your percentage decreases on this shot. The two safest shots are the sharp-angled return and the lob. The lob is particularly good in doubles if the server is coming in behind the serve, and the poacher is playing close to the net as poachers usually do.

I like to poach but don't seem to win many points by doing this. Any advice? You are probably poaching on the wrong shots. Look for the slice or chop returns that have a tendency to rise and float. You might also be letting the ball drop from its high point after crossing the net. The offensive volley is a high to low shot and the higher the impact point above the net, the better.

My partner just will not take advantage of an opponent's weak second serve and advance to the net. What can I do? Under normal circumstances you should both be on the net at every opportunity. However, there may be exceptions. If your opponents are regularly lobbing over you or your partner's head and you can't handle the shot, or if both volleys are not strong, then it might be better to lay back more.

I play a lot of good doubles competition but seem to be getting caught flat-footed on hard serves and some wide balls. Why? One way to speed up your reaction time is to bounce-hop most of the time. However, if you are bouncing too high in the air this could be a factor; keep your feet in motion but close to the ground.

I seem to be getting passed down my alley too often. Any advice? Even great poachers sometimes get passed. However, you might try faking but not going a little more often. If you are still being passed then you are either thinking about something else or your partner is setting you up.

I have a doubles partner who loves to poach and is good at it, but he has a tendency to return to his original spot and we frequently both end up on the same side of the court. Any advice? This can be a problem, but a simple hand signal behind the back helps keep the backcourt person informed. Another simple rule that helps is whenever a ball passes by or over a net person, that person should immediately move to the other side of the court. Also, anyone crossing the center line on a poach, successful or otherwise, should never return to his/her original side until after the point has been concluded.

Chapter 12 Evaluation

1. Discuss the parallel theory used in doubles play.

2. What are the advantages and disadvantages of "Australian Doubles"? How would you attack this system of play?

3. What are the weaknesses of "one up, one back" doubles play?

4. How important is the volley in doubles play?

5. List several points of doubles strategy.

6. Discuss the role of the server in doubles play.

7. What is the best position for you and your partner to play? What chance do you have of winning the point in this position? Why?

8. If you have a rather weak service, what is the most likely place for your partner to play when you are serving?

9. Although this shot is used more in doubles than in singles, it is still called the most under-used shot in the game. What is it? Why do we feel this way?

10. If the server, upon serving, fails to start to the net, what should you as the receiver try to do? Why?

11. Which strokes become more important in doubles than in singles? Why?

12. Briefly discuss the basic responsibilities of players using the "club" doubles system of play.

13. Which player serves first on your team? Why?

14. May I return the service with a volley to achieve a better net position?

15. You have just hit a good lob deep to the backhand corner of your opponent's court. Now what do you and your partner do?

16. Why do we emphasize hitting the ball down the center of the court between our opponents who are at the net?

17. When should my partner (at the net) poach?

18. Which receiver has the most difficult service return in doubles?

19. What are the advantages of "Canadian Doubles"?

20. Are we considered poor sports if we play the weaker opponent? Explain.

Chapter 13

Conditioning for Tennis

Perhaps the first question which needs to be asked is "Why do I want or need to be stronger?" Certainly, if you have aspirations of being a tennis player strength is an asset.

There is sufficient evidence that stronger muscles better protect the joints, thereby decreasing joint injuries. Muscles with greater strength and endurance also are less susceptible to sprains, strains and tears. Another added benefit is that better muscle tone of the trunk muscles decreases the likelihood of low back pain and weak, sagging abdominals.

Additional reasons for maintaining good muscular strength and endurance are less susceptibility to fatigue, faster rehabilitation of muscle injury, better looks, and improvement in feelings of self-confidence and outlook.

A good tennis player needs to be well-conditioned.

QUESTIONS AND ANSWERS ABOUT CONDITIONING

Sometimes I lose large quantities of fluids due to tennis. What is the best replacement? Is there a rule of thumb for replacement? Endurance events lasting longer than 60 minutes will benefit more from a diluted (5-8% carbohydrate) drank because carbohydrates delay the beginning symptoms of exhaustion. The general rule of thumb is to drink fluids equal in volume to that lost by sweating; sixteen fluid ounces are generally considered t be equal to one pound.

Are carbohydrates particularly important to a person who is engaging in heavy exercise? Yes. The average American athlete probably consumes 40-45% of daily calories from fat. Most trainers are now recommending that athletes eat about 70% of total calories in the form of carbohydrates. This serves two important purposes: First, it reduces cholesterol intake and secondly, high carbohydrate diets are particularly important when training or competing on successive days.

Can tennis prevent osteoporosis (loss of bone mass)? Considerable losses of bone mass have been experienced by American and Soviet astronauts who have remained in space for 84 days or more. When bone does not experience normal stress, whether by gravity or inactivity as in the elderly, it will begin to deteriorate. Research, as reported by Shaler, Steel and Carter at Stanford University, indicates that "for bone bass maintenance, it is much more important to have activities with high loads and high stresses than activities with lots of cycles." If they are correct, then tennis should build bone mass. Of course, proper blood calcium levels are necessary and, in some cases, estrogen for women after menopause.

How can I make my muscles grow? Muscle growth is dependent upon three things.

(1) There must be growth stimulation within the body itself at the basic cellular level. After puberty, this is best accomplished by high-intensity exercise.

(2) The proper nutrients must be available for the stimulated cells. Providing large amounts of nutrients in excess of what the body requires will not do anything to promote the growth of muscle fibers. The growth machinery within the cell must be turned on. Muscle stimulation must always precede nutrition. If you stimulate muscular growth by high-intensity exercise, then your muscles will grow on almost any reasonable diet.

(3) The third factor is adequate rest to allow the body time to repair cell damage and to replace the muscle tissue rebuilding ingredients. Actually, the chemical reactions inside a growing muscle are much more complicated than just exercising, eating, and resting. High-intensity muscular contractions result in the formation of a chemical called creatine. This in turn causes the muscle to form more myosin, which enables it to undergo stronger contractions. This in turn causes the production of more creatine, and around we go again.

Remember, you must stimulate growth through high-intensity exercise and then provide the proper nutrients and rest.

How important is physical fitness to good health? While good health and physical fitness are related, it must be noted that regular physical activity does produce some health benefits that are not necessarily directly related to a high degree of physical fitness. For instance, some research studies among adults have shown that exercise on a regular basis is directly related to reduced cases of mental health problems (depression), diabetes, osteoporosis, and certain types of cancer. That regular low-intensity exercise can provide some protection has been further documented by Pfaffenbarger and others in their Harvard alumni study and by Laportes group of researchers.

I am hearing more and more about the dangers of sunburn and skin cancer to tennis players. Any advice? There is no doubt but that excessive sun can cause premature wrinkling, sunburn, and skin cancer. Remember that the hours between 10 AM and 2PM are the worst. Light-colored clothing and a hat will help. However, the best protection against the sun is a sunscreen. Use a SPF (sun protection factor) of about 15 and apply the sunscreen thirty minutes to an hour prior to playing.

How good is tennis as a fitness activity? It really depends upon you and your opponent. If you play singles for at least 30 minutes three times per week *and* against a player equal to or better than yourself, then cardiovascular fitness can be improved. Some people call this "aerobic tennis," and if you work your body at this same level of intensity you can:
— raise your HDL (that's the "good" kind) cholesterol level and lower your total cholesterol level.
— help to control your weight.
— lower your blood pressure.
— relieve psychological stress.

What is the relationship between body fat and very good tennis players? As might be expected, most very good tennis players are not fat. One study of United States, English and Swedish teenage tournament players by Dr. Ben Kibler, a member of the USTA Sport Science Advisory Council, found the boys' body fat range to be 15-18% while the girls' values were from 18-25%. Top male adult players carry about 15%.

What is the most common injury among tennis players? While many part-time players frequently report elbow and forearm injuries, Dr. Kibler believes that rotator cuff (shoulder) tendonitis is the most common injury among tournament-grade players. He believes the key to preventing this injury is to increase the shoulder's ability to stretch.

I have heard a lot about dehydration and how it can cause poor play. What can you tell me about it? One of the most recent studies involved 12 members of the U.S. Junior Wightman Cup team. After five days of training at the Colorado Springs Olympic Training Camp, it was found that several had lost more than seven pounds of water and were approximately 3.75% dehydrated. Since a 2% level of dehydration affects reaction time, speed, and concentration, their performance was definitely below par. Yet each felt she was replacing her daily water loss in an adequate manner.

Are there any foods which cause my body to burn more calories? None that we know of. However, there are foods that can help you cut down on caloric consumption. for instance, one Pennsylvania study indicated that people who eat more soup lose more weight. This particular study found that those who ate soup less than four times per week had a weight loss average of 15% of excess weight. On the other hand, those eating soup four or more times per week had a weight loss average of 20% of excess weight. Another study at Baylor College of Medicine found that soup eaters were more likely to maintain their weight loss after one year. The two factors which probably contribute to the effectiveness of soup are its lower caloric density and the length of time it takes to consume it, particularly if hot.

I try to diet and eat reasonably. However, If I do cheat a little, which food would hurt me least? As Socrates once said, "Moderacy in all things." A little cheating probably won't hurt at all. However, sugar would probably be the least harmful substance assuming you are an active tennis player. The worst are probably high-fat foods and excessive protein. The high-fat foods produce too much cholesterol and decrease the oxygen delivery capability of the body, while excessive protein causes an overaccumulation of uric acid and dehydration. Salt could be a problem if you are bothered by high blood pressure.

If you had to recommend just one vegetable as being the best all-around for nutritional value, what would it be? If you want to get away from calories, then a cup of chopped fresh broccoli fits the bill. For only 45 calories you get about 200% of the daily requirement of Vitamin C, about 25% of your daily fiber needs, about 90% of daily Vitamin A needs, 10% each of calcium, phosphorus, and thiamin, about 8% of iron, 6% of niacin, some potassium, and about 8% of your daily protein requirement. Not bad for one vegetable! In addition, some researchers believe broccoli is one of the vegetables that may protect us against certain forms of cancer.

Is there a simple rule of thumb for determining how many calories a person needs each day? You might try this simple guideline used by many people:

— Very Active: If you are a very active person, you might eat 25 calories per pound of your body weight and remain the same weight.

— Moderately Active: You might need up to 20 calories per pound to stay constant.

— Lightly Active: A lightly active person might need as many as 15 calories per pound of body weight to remain the same weight.

— Very Inactive: A very inactive person will need only about 10-12 calories per pound to remain at the same weight.

Remember that while "total" calories are important, a balanced caloric intake is probably more important to all-around total health.

What can you tell me about "tennis elbow"? Aside from the advice that we hope you don't get it, physicians say there are two types: lateral (outside) and medial (inside) with the outside kind being about five times more common. The problem is microscopic tears in muscles and tendons that control your wrist and fingers. The site of pain is where the tendons attach in the elbow. Causes are generally poor technique and/or overuse. Other possibilities include tight strings, playing with wet and heavy tennis balls, and sometimes excessively heavy or light tennis rackets. The poor technique that gets most people in trouble is leading with the elbow. Anticipating the next question, use rest, ice and aspirin or other over-the-counter medications.

How prevalent is "tennis elbow"? One study, as reported by *Tennis* magazine, indicated that 20% of surveyed respondents had elbow problems. Also, most were using a light-weight racket at the time of injury. Most doctors will tell you to rest. However, whether you rest the elbow or not, you should probably stay away from the very stiff rackets such as graphite, boron and steel. If you have a really bad elbow, try using a wood racket.

How will I know when I am warmed up? How long should the warm-up take? The time will vary with the person, but usually there is a feeling of well-being and readiness which comes over us as the warm-up progresses. However, if you want something more solid, you should be ready when you break into a good sweat. The amount of time that it takes to do this will depend upon the temperature, the humidity of the air, and the intensity of your warm-up.

Is there any harm in "grunting" each time I hit the ball? It is generally conceded that excessive grunting can cause symptoms of hyperventilation. The release of too much carbon dioxide produces difficulty in breathing, numbness in hands muscle tightening and sometimes chest pain. If you grunt a lot and are experiencing these symptoms try breathing in and out of a closely-held paper bag.

I am prone to muscle tears. Is there anything I can do? Some players have pulled muscles just by stretching. If you are in this category, try raising your body temperature before you do your stretching exercises. This can best be done by piling on a few extra layers of clothing or taking a hot shower or both before doing warm-up exercises.

Should there be any difference in my warm-up before playing on cold days? Most authorities believe that stretching cold muscles on a cold day leads to injuries. They suggest very light exercises to warm the muscles. Then do your stretching.

What are the most common medical problems of tennis players? The following problems seem to plague tennis players from time to time. We have therefore included them so you can become familiar with them and prepare yourself appropriately.

SPRAINED ANKLE

Ankle sprains are one of the most common injuries of tennis. The injury usually involves damage to ligaments and tendons surrounding the joint and/or to the capsule-like sac surrounding the joint. Severe ankle sprains may not be distinguishable from a fracture (except by x-ray) and may take longer to heal. However, there are procedures that, if followed, will minimize pain and speed recovery. These are:

1. Stop activity—take weight off foot.
2. Elevate leg and apply an elastic (Ace) bandage, taking care that you do not apply the bandage so tightly that circulation to the foot is cut off.
3. Apply ice water or cold packs until swelling is stabilized.

Restoration of flexibility should begin after the damaged ligaments, tendons, and capillaries have healed. At that time begin by moving the ankle through its entire range of motion several times daily. Applying pressure with the side of your foot to a chair helps also. Later, try filling a sock with sand and placing it across the foot before doing a wide range of motion.

184

Taping or wrapping before the ankle strength is fully restored is usually a sound preventive measure. However, after full recover most authorities recommend removal of supports so that a full strengthening of the limb can occur.

BLISTERS

Tennis is a game of sudden starts and stops. Obviously, this entails great wear and tear upon the feet and frequently results in blisters. Pre-season jogging, wearing two pairs of socks, keeping the feet dry and wearing properly fitted shoes will usually help in preventing the problem. However, when a blister does occur there are two choices. Leave it alone and the fluids will eventually be absorbed by the body. The other choice is to scrub thoroughly with soap and water, then sterilize a needle over an open flame and make a small opening at the base or back part of the blister. Drain the fluid and apply a sterile dressing. If you must continue to play, a small felt or sponge rubber pad with a hole (doughnut) cut in the center will offer some protection by taking the pressure off of that particular spot. If you are prone to hand blisters, they can sometimes be prevented by the use of a tennis glove.

MUSCLE CRAMPS

Cramps are sudden involuntary muscle contractions causing great pain. They may occur at any time and are characterized by repeated contractions and relaxations or sometimes as a steady continuous muscle contraction. Their causes are varied; however, fatigue, loss of body fluids and minerals, and the accumulation of waste products within the muscles are all contributing factors. Rest and replenishment of body fluids and salts will usually remedy the problem.

MUSCLE PULLS AND TEARS

This disability is usually caused by lack of flexibility and excessive stress. One of the most common muscle tears occurs in the calf muscle. When this injury occurs, there is immediate sharp pain within the heavy part of the calf. Swelling usually occurs within a few hours and the area may become black and blue within several days. Walking, running, or rising on the toes is painfully difficult. Immediate application of cold packs and resting the leg will usually help. Later on, applications of moist heat, massage, and gradual usage will hasten recovery.

BACK PAIN

Back pain is a reasonably common occurrence among part-time and fulltime athletes. The most common cause is postural—i.e., shortened hamstring and back muscles accompanied by weak abdominal muscles. Bent knee situps accompanied by stretching exercises for the back and hamstring muscles will usually prevent or lessen this injury. However, once back pain occurs, the best treatment is rest. Application of heat will sometimes help but one must be careful to limit the application to small amounts of time at a low setting. Too much heat will increase irritation and swelling, thus causing more pain. *Do not* fall asleep on a heating pad.

TIPS ON CONDITIONING

1. Understand the components of "being fit" for tennis, then seek to develop each component maximally. These components are: flexibility, agility, muscular strength and endurance, cardio-pulmonary endurance, power, coordination, reaction time.

2. Determine a program of training that is apart from your time on the court in skill practice. Establish areas of prominence in your fitness needs and how they relate to the demands of the game. Begin a worthwhile program.

3. Use progression. Start with the simple and slowly build. It takes time, but not so much as you might imagine.

4. Establish an optimistic outlook. Think positively toward the rewards you know will be forthcoming. Think like a winner!

5. Establish routines that enhance footwork, especially since the importance of this part of the game is recognized.

CHAPTER 13 EVALUATION

1. Explain your attitude towards the warm-up as you have always taken it.

2. What elements should a proper warm-up include? What time factor is involved?

3. There are many conditioning programs that are available to almost everyone. Which style will fit your *needs* best? Remember, it is not just how much time you have but how much time should be spent?

4. List those items you would include in *your* exercise and training program.

5. What are *your* realistic goals for your tennis career?

6. What are your needs (physically) and how can they help you in attaining your goal?

7. The normal warm-up is sufficient in most cases for tennis match participation. True or false?

8. Make a detailed written plan for your warm-up program.

9. If you established a training program for yourself that was all-inclusive, what you would include in it?

10. Will your cardiovascular program aid your footwork? Explain.

11. When considering proper foods, as a tennis player you should be aware of those which can cause a decrease in oxygen delivery to the body. Which foods are these?

12. Name a common treatment for "tennis elbow." What are the causes?

13. If you suffer a muscle pull, which treatment should you utilize first?

Practice Drills

Tennis drills should be progressive in nature. There are no short-cuts in learning skill patterns. A student of the game should first seek professional instruction which will set the pace, determine the course, and generate interest in achieving one's potential. The tennis instructor should then establish drills and patterns for practice. Many of these drills will be "dry" drills, using no balls but simply going through the stroking pattern to learn the sequence and to train the muscles in acquiring the new skill.

Practically speaking, drills are divided into four general areas:

1. Footwork drills
2. Basic instructional drills
3. Skill drills
4. Advanced competitive drills

Each group is divided into many drills that are progressive in nature, and easy to understand.

SELECTED FOOTWORK DRILLS

It has been said, and reliably so, that footwork is about 60% of the game of tennis. This being the case, it becomes obvious that this fundamental must be developed to the maximum level. Each serious student of the game should have a practice plan which will achieve maximum results. The following footwork patterns have been selected because of their aggressiveness, practicality, and conditioning benefits. No balls are actually hit in any of these footwork drills.

Jump rope. Use primarily a single hop; may be done on both feet, or either one. Jumping rope can be very useful also as a conditioner. Several patterns and styles can be used.

Crossover step. Punch volley each step. Begin in a ready position, then use a cross-step (forward pivot) to the forehand and to the backhand in quick repetition, hitting an imaginary volley each time. Emphasis is on speed and correct footwork pattern. Do four to six thirty-second rounds.

Serve and go. Begin at the baseline, without use of tennis balls. Serve and go to the net, using a check-stop at the service line and continuing to the net. Repeat many times.

Zig zag run. From center mark, place balls in an irregular pattern on either side. Using a broken pattern, proceed to each ball on the ground and stroke each imaginary ball at the location of the ball on the ground.

Up the alley. Using the cross-step pattern already described, begin at the baseline on one side of the alley. Use the pattern to cross and punch an imaginary volley, continuing to move forward each step. Continue until you go "up the alley." Execution should be rapid and footwork should be correct. Do approximately six rounds.

Up and over. Start at the singles sideline. Begin by moving forward to the service line then stop and hit an imaginary ground stroke, then go along the service line to the midcourt line, stop an hit a ground stroke, go up the midcourt line to the net, punch a volley, then go to the side—right or left—extend (stretch) to hit the final volley. Go to the opposite side of the baseline and begin again. Go through five times.

Side step drill. Place yourself halfway between the midcourt line and singles sideline. Using a side skipping motion, move to a point that will allow you to stroke a ball at the singles sideline, pivot and stroke. Then rapidly recover and move to the midcourt line and execute a stroke, repeat for 30 seconds. Then start again. Continue for four to six repetitions.

Jog and stroke. Starting at court #1 on your court complex, begin to jog around the courts. Check stop every five steps and stroke a forehand or a backhand, alternating with each stop. Continue around the courts.

Shuttle run. Place four balls on the court equidistant from the baseline to the net. Begin by running, racket in hand, to the first ball, return to the baseline running backwards, then go to the second ball. Continue to the baseline backwards, then on to the third, etc., until you go to all four balls. Repeat three times.

Quick step and volley. Spread out on the court. Begin running in place. On every tenth step quickly execute a forehand volley, recover and continue to run in place; then a backhand volley is hit. Continue this routine for thirty seconds or more. This can be done easily with a partner using hand signals—you move to the side according to whether partner lifts right or left arm quickly. Be alert. Continue to move the feet at all times.

Sundial. From your position on the court, place seven balls eight feet from you, representing the hours on the face of a clock. Begin the exercise by stepping and stretching to reach the ball, using correct footwork for the side of the body on which the ball is located.

BASIC INSTRUCTIONAL DRILLS

THE FOREHAND   *Repetitions*

1. From a ready position, obtain the "shake hands" grip. Release, repeat.   10
2. From a ready position, try the forward pivot, check foot position, recover.   10
3. Repeat # 2 using the reverse pivot.   10
4. Using the forward pivot, take the complete backswing. Check height of the racket hand.   10
5. Using the forward pivot, combine the backswing, forward swing and follow-through in one smooth, flowing motion.   10
6. From the back of the court, turn your left side to the fence. Drop a ball in *front* of the left side and stroke the ball into the fence twenty feet away. Recover the ready position, then repeat. Now hit the ball over the net.   25
7. Drop a ball as in #6 and stroke it to a rebound wall. Catch ball, drop and repeat.   25
8. Repeat #7, keeping the ball to the right half of the forward rebound wall and above the three-foot net line.   20
9. Repeat #8, keeping the ball in play to the right half of the forward rebound wall.   20
10. Try to replay the rebound against the forward wall (number of bounces is not important at the stage).   30

PARTNER DRILLS: FOREHAND   *Repetitions*

11. Have a partner toss from the net (center) to
    a circle just behind the service line. Stroke
    using full pivot.   30
12. Toss from net into a circle just above the baseline,
    stroke from baseline into opponent's court. Use
    full pivot.   30
13. Repeat #12, except substitute a ball machine
    for tosser. Hit three baskets of balls apiece.   3
14. Repeat #13. Aim each ball to the opposite side of
    opponent's court from the last ball (check
    fundamentals).   3
15. Drop a ball and stroke to your partner on the opposite
    side of the net. Try to continue a forehand rally.   30 minutes

If you detect any trouble with the forehand, go back and review the fundamentals. Acquire a good mental picture of what you are after. If you *understand* it, it will greatly assist you in skill development.

As in the forehand, the drills listed below are in progressive order from the simple to the complex. If you use these drills, take your time and go slowly. The number of repetitions should be used as a guide only. You may need fewer, or more, depending on your particular progress.

THE BACKHAND   *Repetitions*

1. From a ready position, change from a forehand
   grip to a backhand grip.   10
2. Repeat #1, and use the forward pivot to the left side
   changing grips as you execute the pivot. Check footwork
   positions.   10
3. Repeat #2, only use the reverse pivot, stepping back
   rather than forward.   10
4. Using the forward pivot, take the racket back in to the full
   backswing position. Check the height of racket head
   (keep low).   10
5. Repeat #4, and add the forward swing and follow-through.
   Go very slowly, check racket head position. Lead with the
   head of racket.   15

BACKHAND, *Continued*   *Repetitions*

6. From the back of the court area turn your right side to the
    fence, drop a ball in front of the right side and execute a
    backhand stroke to the fence, twenty feet away. Recover
    and repeat.   25
7. Drop a ball and stroke it to a rebound wall. Catch the ball
    and repeat.   25
8. Repeat #7, except aim the ball above an imaginary
    three-foot line representing the tennis net.   25
9. Repeat #8, keeping the ball to the left side of the front wall. 20
10. Try to replay the rebound against the forward wall
    (number of bounces is not important now).   20

PARTNER DRILLS: BACKHAND   *Repetitions*

11. Have a partner toss from the center of the net into
    a small circle behind the service line. Stroke, using a full
    backhand stroke with pivot, adjusting the toss to the circle.   30
12. Toss from the net into a circle just above the baseline.
    Stroke from the baseline into the opponent's court.
    Use full pivot.   30
13. Repeat #12, except substitute ball machine for tosser.
    Hit at least three trays of balls each.   3+
14. Repeat #13, aiming each ball to the opposite side of
    opponent's court from the last ball. Check fundamentals.   3
15. Drop a ball and stroke to your partner on the opposite
    side to the net. Try to continue a backhand rally.   30 minutes
16. Using both forehand and backhand, drop a ball and
    keep a rally going as long as possible. Continue until
    your continuous count totals 1,000 shots hit over the net.

    You have now completed the two basic strokes in tennis. If there is
a problem you cannot handle, contact your instructor, or go back and
read and repeat your skill progressions. When you have completed
the work on the backhand stroke, review the skill and knowledge
objectives to determine if further emphasis is needed.

194

THE SERVICE   *Repetitions*

1. Practice the coordination of swing for both arms.
   Right arm to backswing and left arm toward ball toss.
   Shift weight back as arms begin movement.
   Do not toss the ball.   20
2. Practice the toss of the ball, noticing the height
   and where it lands on the court.   30
3. Repeat #1, tossing ball up as racket arm is taken back.
   Do not hit the ball.   25
4. Repeat #3. Face the fence, and serve into the fence,
   work on ball toss, contact point, and height.   30
5. At service line, serve five good serves diagonally
   across to correct service court.   5
6. Repeat #5, except move back one yard after each time
   after five good serves, gradually working your way to
   the baseline.   5+
7. *From the baseline,* using the correct form, serve ten
   to right court, then ten to left court. Repeat.   20+
8. Serve 20 flat serves into the right service court.
9. Serve 20 flat serves into the left service court.
10. Serve 100 balls to each service court, R + L.   200
11. Divide the opposite service courts into quarters.
    Serve 25 balls to each area.
    Area #1—Forehand corner for receiver, *Right service court*
    Area #2—Backhand corner for receiver, *Right service court*
    Area #3—Forehand corner for receiver, *Left service court*
    Area #4—Backhand corner for receiver, *Left service court*
    As you continue to practice, aim the ball to either area 1 or 2,
    or area 3 or 4, depending on which side you are serving from.
    Remember to always serve *diagonally across* the court.
12. Repeat #10, but serve 50 serves to each area
    (one through four) in numerical order.   200

Increase your speed only as you are able to maintain control and placement.

THE VOLLEY   *Repetitions*

1. From proper net position, have partner toss balls
   to your forehand, from service line. Volley back to
   your partner. Keep toss chest high, toss overhand.   30
2. Repeat #1, except now use the backhand volley.   30
3. Alternating forehand and backhand volley, hit from
   toss back to partner. Toss overhand.   50
4. Forehand only, vary height of the toss. Direct volley
   toward partner if possible.   50
5. Repeat #4 using the backhand.   30
6. Repeat #3; aim ball to opposite corner of opponent's court. 30
7. Repeat #4; aim ball to opposite corner of opponent's court. 30
8. Using a ball machine, alternate loads to the forehand and
   backhand, two rounds of balls to each side.   4
9. Using the same machine, from the same tossing position
   move from the baseline, stroking the ball to the opponent's
   backhand; then as you move to the net, volley the next ball.
   (Repeat: 10 approach shots and 10 volleys.)   20
10. Have baseline partner stroke a ball to you at the net, then
    volley the ball back to partner for another ground stroke.
    Feed the ball to each other.   20

THE SMASH   *Repetitions*

1. Obtain the correct grip, turn to the left side of the net
   in the forecourt area, and exercise the full swing
   without the ball.   10
2. Toss to the baseline to the partner at the net (forecourt).
   Smash the ball at half speed into the opponent's court. 30
3. Repeat #2, but begin aiming the ball at different angles
   (left, right, short, deep).   20
4. Repeat #2, but aim the ball to the opponent's deep
   backcourt area.   20
5. Have partner lob the ball to you with his/ her racket.
   Execute the smash to varying areas of opponent's courts. 20

SKILL DRILLS

Most skill drills are part of an intensive practice plan. There are drills for each stroke, often using a partner to feed the ball. Three drill areas are basic to good tennis and should be practiced on a regular basis. These areas are:
1. Serve and return of serve.
2. Groundstroke consistency and accuracy from the baseline.
3. Placement of passing shots.

Also, additional time should be given to the accomplishment of the support strokes, or those which complement the basic game. These areas are:
1. Combination of serve and volley.
2. Use of the approach shot.
3. The volley and net tactics.
4. The overhead or smash.
5. Offensive and defensive lobs.

Time should be allowed for practice and play, with neither partner totally dominating the other. Some selected drill skills are as follows.
1. Rally from the backcourt area at the center mark.
2. Stroke crosscourt shots—both backhand and forehand rallies.
3. Use an "X" drill. One partner hits crosscourt only while the other partner hits down the line only.
4. Two partners face each other near the sideline. One hits forehands down the line and the partner hits backhands. They hit to each other.
5. One partner has a basket of balls at service line. Hit balls to partner running partner from corner to corner.
6. Serve only—to both forehand and backhand service courts.
7. One partner at the net, one at the baseline—rally.
8. Same as #7, using only forehand or only backhand.
9. One partner at net, one at baseline, volley and lob practice.
10. Using a feeder, hit forehand or backhand volleys only.
11. Overheads, feed setups from the baseline.
12. Volley-rally-overhead drill. One partner at the net, other at the baseline. The net player hits a volley, then an overhead from the drive, and then the lob fed by the baseliner.
13. Hit overhead, touch net, hit overhead, and touch net; continue 10 times. Feeder is partner at the baseline.
14. Four-ball drill: Hit from baseline, half-volley at service line, volley at net and overhead. Feeder is partner at the baseline.

15. Serve and lob return drill. Basic practice for doubles, good change of pace drill.
16. Serve or return serve to target area. Use tennis balls or cans as targets.
17. Angled volley to backhand cones—either side. Feeder at center of baseline. Basket of balls to each partner. Feeder may move along baseline to create different angles.
18. Both partners at net—volley from the service line, keeping the ball in play.
19. Same as #18 only use crosscourt volley.
20. Volley rally against a wall.
21. Three-player volley drill: All players at the service line, keeping one ball in play. Change places frequently.
22. "X" drill with one player at the net volleying crosscourt only, while partner at the baseline hits ground strokes down the line only. Both players keep ball within reach of partner but requires extensive movement. May vary at random.

COMPETITIVE DRILLS

These drills may use a point system to encourage a "game-like" situation. Practice should be intense and care should be taken not to make careless errors. Most drills are aggressive and demand skill competency.

1. Serve and return of serve. One player *serves only*, and his/her partner works on service *returns only*. Vary serves and returns, concentrating on effective strategy in each area. Alternate using both courts, and rotate players.
2. Serve and play out point. The server moves into net and the players involved play the point to completion.
3. Serve and follow serve to the net (use check stop). Server continues service motion and heads to net. Pause momentarily to utilize the check stop before moving to the ball. Alternate right and left service courts.
4. Serve or go to net—service return cannot bounce on server's side. Server moves to the net immediately, closing in so that the return is not allowed to bounce. Utilizing a game situation may increase motivation.
5. Serve—only one serve per point—and play point. Server is only allowed one service per point. This way, more care is taken toward making the service good.

6. Volley—two at the net—slow to fast—use point system. Both players stand at the service line. Keep the ball in play between partners. Increase speed of the volley as control can be maintained. Use a point system ("21") to increase motivation and court coverage. Use halfcourt area from side to side (center service line to sideline).

7. Volley—to baseline rally—try to pass opponent at net. One player at the net, partner at the baseline. Baseliner feeds partner at the net, slowly increasing the tempo until passing shots are used.

8. Volley—only to forehand or backhand side. Try to pass. Volley goes down the line only. Use the center service line as a guide for the net player and the center mark for the baseliner. Each player goes "down the line" only, but recovers to the line or mark between strokes. Go for winners.

9. Volley—four at net—keep one ball going. All four begin at the service line and move into the net as able. Each player should attempt to keep the volley/half-volley low, causing the opponent to hit up on the shot to clear the net.

10. Two vs. one at the baseline. One tries to pass two at the net. The two players at the net cover the doubles area, the baseliner covers the singles court only. Attempt to volley the ball so the baseliner must "cover" the baseline area completely. However, discretion is necessary as the net players can easily win the point, thus defeating the purpose of the drill. Change every five minutes. Lobs allowed only at discretion of the coach.

11. Two vs. one at the net. Two try to pass one at the net. Reverse the drill described in #10 above. Baseliners (two) attempt to pass the volleyer (one). Lobs allowed at discretion of the coach.

12. Protect your partner—doubles set-up—use rally—attempt to poach. This three-player drill uses a server, receiver, and the server's partner. Each player practices each area, including poaching. Rotate every five minutes. Use right and left service courts.

13. Serve and lob return to backhand quarter of court. This doubles drill is excellent for (1) serving practice and (2) utilizing the lob return of service. Practice the lob over the head of an imaginary net player. Use a bucket of balls for each player.

14. Return serve to target area on court. Place targets on the court at strategic areas. While the server practices the service, the receiver concentrates on placement on the service return to a selected target area.
15. Serve to target on service court. Place cans, balls, paper targets at critical service areas on the service court, selected to facilitate a weak return or an ace. Practice serving a bucket of balls to these areas.
16. Depth rally—hit to backcourt area only—use point system. Players remain at the baseline, stroke the ball into the backcourt area between the service line and the baseline. Players may accumulate points by various scoring methods. Games and sets may be played using this drill.
17. Long rally—count the number of hits between partners—try for best score—one bounce. Players must strive to keep the ball in play without an error. Stroke the ball deep to the backcourt area. No attempt is made to hit winners. This drill is excellent for developing consistency.
18. Consecutive volleys from inside service line. Count score. Players use a volley rally drill, keeping the ball at moderate speed. Count is maintained to see which team can accumulate the longest continuous rally.
19. Volley rally vs. rebound wall. Number of volleys in one minute. Stand about 12 feet from rebound wall and keep the ball in play using the volley only. Use 30-second to one-minute segments. Can be easily adaptable to competition.
20. "King of the Court." Singles. Play first to reach 10 points, rotate serve. Winner moves one court toward #1 court, loser stays. Loser on #1 goes to bottom and starts over (singles and doubles).
21. Use serve and attempt to approach the net. Halfcourt game of 21—lengthwise. All shots must be within half-court area. Put-away smash= 3 points, volley = 2 points, all others = 1 point. Rotate serve each 5 points. Use serve and attempt to approach the net.
22. Lob rally—4 players—2 deep, 2 at net within service line. Net players put away all short lobs. If lob is behind the service court, the net player must allow the ball to be played by the baseliner behind him/her.

23. Four-ball drill five times. Count number of balls in the court. Begin at the baseline. Player is fed a deep shot for rally, short ball for an approach, a volley at the net and a lob for an overhead. Feeder makes no attempt to play the returned balls, but feeds from a basket of balls. Rotate after five trials.

24. Short game using service courts only. This game utilizes good footwork and is primarily fun oriented but demands ball control. The value in actual game situations is limited.

25. Figure Eight drill using full court. Two players attempt to keep the ball in play using crosscourt strokes only on one side of the net, and down the line strokes only on the other. This is an aggressive drill demanding skill and stamina. It can be used with one deep and one at the net using the same directions. However, attempts are made not to put the ball away, but to extend the partner maximally.

CHAPTER 14 EVALUATION

1. List and diagram two individual drills for each of the following: forehand, backhand, service, volley, and lob.

2. List and diagram two "partner drills" for the above shots.

3. What is "progression" and how important is it to the development of skill proficiency?

4. In your own words, tell why "backboards" are good practice devices for intermediate and advanced players, but are not so appropriate for beginners.

5. Why are drills so good for the serious player as well as the weekender?

Chapter 15

Tournaments and Officiating

There are so many different types of tournaments—some are short, others lengthy. Several types are continuous—that is, never ending. Five of the most popular tournaments will be discussed in this chapter: pyramid, ladder, round robin, single elimination, and double elimination.

THE PYRAMID TOURNAMENT

The pyramid tournament is used frequently in clubs and camps. It is one of those types of tournament that has no ending place, unless time is placed upon the entrants. The pyramid tournament has a large capacity, generally accommodating forty to fifty players.

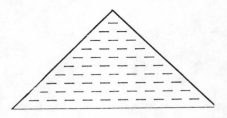

The Pyramid Tournament Board

SYSTEM OF PLAY

** Each line "_" is about an inch in length.

** Place a name on each line in the pyramid.

** The objective of the tournament is to reach the top space, then to defend it against all challengers.

** Players may challenge up one line at a time—best of 3 sets (or pro-sets).

** If the challenged player is defeated, he/she changes places with the victor. If the challenged player wins, the position is not changed.

** Players may challenge up only one line at a time. The challenged player must respond to the challenge within one week or default. The time is to be arranged by both players involved.

** This type of tournament allows the challenger to select the style of play best suited to his/her game, thus adding to the chances of success.

THE LADDER TOURNAMENT

Ladder tournaments are fun and add excitement when time limits are placed on the entrants. The structure of the ladder is just as the name implies—it is in the form of a ladder. This tournament is used frequently by clubs and tennis teams to determine the ranking of players representing the group; the ladder tournament is designed so that the players participate enough times to allow a ranking to take place. The best player ends up at the top spot, followed by the second best, etc.

The Ladder Tournament

SYSTEM OF PLAY

Rank the players to the best of your ability in the space above. Begin in Round #1, with the player on line 1 vs the player on line 2, line 3 vs line 4, etc. If the number of players is uneven, the bottom player does not have a match this time. Remember, in Round #1 the even numbers challenge up; in round 2, the odd numbers challenge up (see the diagram).

If the higher-ranked player wins the match, he/she keeps the higher position. If the lower-ranked player wins, he/she changes places with the higher player. When Round #2 begins, the top-ranked player does not play, since the player on line 2 must play down this time. (Odd numbers challenge up!)

Players may challenge only one line up at a time. This is usually arranged by the instructor, coach or tennis pro.

In order for a ladder tournament to be successful, 10 to 15 rounds should be played, as the ladder changes structure frequently. This many rounds will allow the ladder to become somewhat stabilized.

This tournament will produce an accurate lineup for future matches or ranking in the club.

THE ROUND ROBIN TOURNAMENT

Round Robin tournaments are used when plenty of time is available, as each contestant must play all the others. If there are ten players in the tournament, each player must play the other nine entries. This will take many courts and offer the tournament director a fine tournament to run over many days. The winner is usually the player who has the highest percentage of wins at the conclusion of the matches. In case of a tie, the two leaders should play a match to determine the winner.

A round robin tournament must be scheduled carefully in order to eliminate confusion.

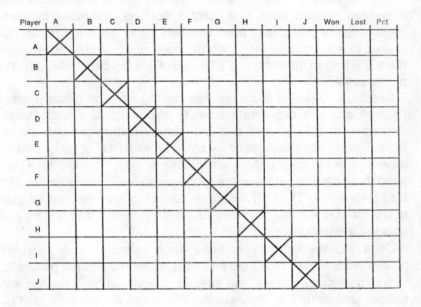

The Round Robin Tournament

Playing rounds are scheduled below:

# 1	# 2	# 3	# 4	# 5	# 6	# 7	# 8	#9
A VS J	A VS I	A VS H	A VS G	A VS F	A VS E	A VS D	A VS C	A VS B
B VS I	J VS H	I VS G	H VS F	G VS E	F VS D	E VS C	D VS B	C VS J
C VS H	B VS G	J VS F	I VS E	H VS D	G VS C	F VS B	E VS J	D VS I
D VS G	C VS F	B VS E	J VS D	I VS C	H VS B	G VS J	F VS I	E VS H
E VS F	D VS E	C VS D	B VS C	J VS B	I VS J	H VS I	G VS H	F VS G

(Notice the "system" in the rotation used above.)

SINGLE ELIMINATION TOURNAMENTS

Tournament Size. A single elimination tournament must be a multiple of two, so that it is equal on both top and bottom. A tournament of this type must be either a draw of 4, 8, 16, 32, 64, 128, etc. Most tournaments do not go larger than 32 entries due to the necessity for completion within a reasonable time. Probably the most common is a 16 draw (entry). Larger tournaments (district, state or national) may easily be 64 to 128 draw, depending on their importance. For a weekend, a 16 draw is almost ideal.

The tournament director must remember that a tournament may draw men, women, boys, girls, singles, doubles, and mixed doubles. Each of these demands a tournament in itself. Thus the number of entries in each tournament, plus the number of courts and whether there are lighted facilities, and time, will play a big part in the success of the event.

Seeding. Seeding is simply determining who the better players (teams) are and separating them to make a better tournament. According to USTA rules, the Tournament Committee determines the seeds, selecting one seed for every four entries, or major portion thereof. For example, if there are thirteen entries, the committee may seed three players. If there are fourteen entries, either three or four may be seeded. The USTA Section governing your area will be glad to provide you with specific rules for seeding. They are important and should be followed.

Once the seeded players have been selected, they must be placed in the draw. There are exact places for them to go; generally, in a sixteen draw, the first two seeded players will go in the top and bottom spaces on the draw sheet. Who goes where is decided by the flip of a coin or names are drawn out of a hat. The three and four seeds will go at spaces five and twelve; follow the same procedure to determine which player goes to each area.

Placing the "Byes." A bye is simply an empty space in the draw sheet. The bye is needed when you have fewer players than you have on the draw sheet. For example, if you have thirteen entries in your tournament, you must use a sixteen-space draw sheet. Since you do not have enough players to fill it, you will be left with three byes. They go in specific spaces as outlined in the rules. The word "bye" is placed in the space rather than leaving it blank. The player opposing a "bye" proceeds to the next round without playing in the first round. All "byes" are eliminated in the first round.

2. _____

3. _____

4. _____

The Single Elimination Tournament

In placing the byes in the draw, the first bye goes in the open space at the bottom of the draw sheet (15), the second bye goes in the first open space in the top (2), the third in the bottom (13) and the fourth in the top (4) and so forth, using this sequence.

Making the Draw. Once the seeds and byes have been placed on the draw sheet, the next procedure to follow is to draw the remaining names out of the hat. They are drawn out one name at a time, and placed on the draw beginning with the first open space at the top, and continuing downward in the order in which they are drawn. If the draw has been made correctly, there are no empty spaces nor are there any leftover names.

Assigning the Times to Play. Now that you have completed the draw, assign the times for the participants to play and assign courts, if possible. You are then ready for the matches to begin.

Remember:

1. Tournament size is a multiple of 2 (4, 8, 16, 32, 64).
2. One seed for every four entries.
3. Seeds go at 1, 16, 5, and 12, in that order.
4. Byes, if needed, begin at 15, then 2, 13, 4, 11, etc., in that order.
5. Place times on the sheet to assist players and tournament managers.

THE DOUBLE ELIMINATION TOURNAMENT

A double elimination tournament means just that—you must lose twice before you are out of the tournament. Although this seems to be more favorable for all participants, it is not often used in tournament play. The main reason for this is the lack of time available for tournament play (usually only weekends) and the additional time it takes to play the double elimination bracket.

The tournament is drawn up the same as the single elimination tournament, except a loser's bracket is added on the left side of the draw sheet. Thus, when a player loses on the right (winner's) side, he/she moves to the loser's (left) side at approximately the same place in the tournament.

The double elimination tournament meets with the approval of most contestants because, though a player has lost one round, he/she is still in the tournament and could eventually win. Double elimination tournaments are best used for small groups of players (8 or less) where time is not a consideration.

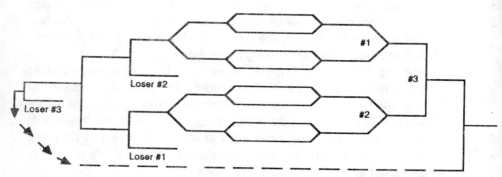

This winner moves over to the winner's side and plays again.

Double Elimination Tournament

OFFICIATING

The responsibility of officials at tennis events is not easy. Most often officials are a carefully selected group of dedicated men and women who have a deep interest in the sport. They often sacrifice their desire to watch the game from the grandstand to serve in an official position of the court. Their job is not an easy one, for they sometimes are harassed by spectators or players, and being human, they can make an occasional mistake. However, abuse and mistakes are relatively rare, and the official enjoys a position of importance and serves as an instrument of smooth match operation.

There are three officials used in tournament matches. They are (1) the referee, (2) the umpire, and (3) the linesman. Each has separate responsibilities which are described below:

THE REFEREE

Appointed by the Tournament Committee.

The Referee shall be a member of the committee.

Shall make the draw, assisted by the committee.

Supervises all aspect of play, including conduct of players, umpires, ball boys, ground crew, etc.

Shall appoint a deputy when he or she is away from his or her post.

May default players for reasonable causes.

Acts as final judge on appeals of defaulted players.

Schedules matches, assigns courts, suspends play, etc., according to conditions.

In summation, the referee is in **total control of the tournament.**

THE UMPIRE (Chair Umpire)

Shall conduct the match according to the rules of tennis.

Shall assume the duties of all linesmen not present.

May ask for the replacement of linesmen, if needed.

Sees that players on his/her court follow all rules of match play.

May order a replay of a point if linesmen are unable to make a call.

Shall advise the referee of unfavorable court or match conditions.

Shall decide any point of law (rules) concerning the match.

May default a player for cause.

THE LINESMAN (Line Umpire)

Call all shots relating to the lines he/she is assigned; decisions are **final.**

Shall promptly indicate by unsighted signal when he/she is unable to make a call.

Shall only at the chair umpire's request render a firm opinion on a shot observed in an area outside his/her responsibility.

Shall call foot faults pertaining to his/her line, as outlined in the Rules.

The only other official found on the court is the net umpire, whose primary responsibility is to call a "let" serve. This person may also keep an additional score card as a backup to the chair umpire.

Thus, we see that as an organized sport, a logical chain-of-command is used to assure a smooth, efficiently-run athletic event. This is assured by selecting knowledgeable, qualified and experienced personnel to assist the tournament committee in the organization and administration of the tournament. An experienced player should know, recognize and appreciate the responsibilities of all tournament officials. They are, after all, working for the players.

Linesman   Chair Umpire   Net Umpire

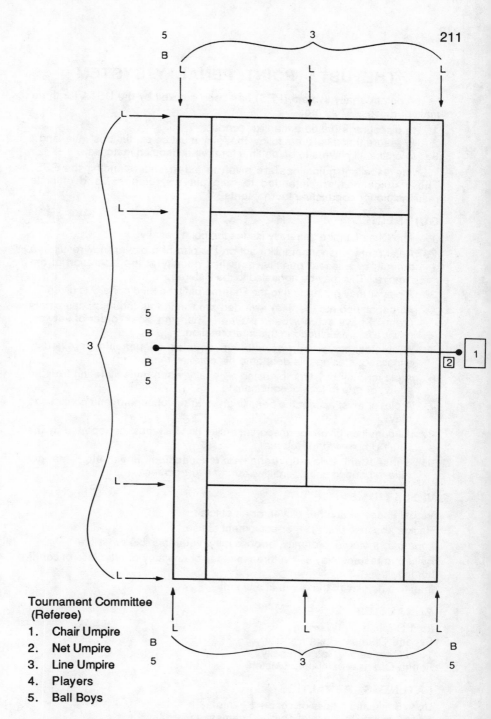

Tournament Committee
(Referee)

1. Chair Umpire
2. Net Umpire
3. Line Umpire
4. Players
5. Ball Boys

In singles, the linesmen will be positioned on the singles side boundaries instead of the doubles boundaries shown here.

THE TOURNAMENT CHAIN-OF-COMMAND

THE USTA POINT PENALTY SYSTEM

The point penalty system (PPS) has been devised by the USTA for three main purposes. They are:

1. to discourage unsportsmanlike conduct,
2. to assure that all players follow the "play must be continuous" rule, and
3. to entice all players to be on time for their scheduled matches.

Some excellent guidelines are given to aid in understanding the PPS. These guidelines are intended to help players, umpires, and officials responsible for conducting tournaments.

GUIDELINES

1. The Chair Umpire generally issues the point penalty.
2. A flagrantly unsportsmanlike act on the part of a player may result in a default, or a lesser penalty, as a first penalty at the discretion of the Umpire. This may be appealed to the Referee.
3. A player may not appeal to the Referee until the third penalty is given.
4. All penalty points (games) awarded are treated as though those points (games) have actually been played. Changing sides, order of service, new balls are included in this interpretation.
5. A singles player carries into his doubles all penalties previously assessed, placing this debt onto his doubles team.
6. A player may buy time by using a penalty when he is suffering from an injury, or due to lack of conditioning.
7. A player must accept the penalty given to the opponent, and continue to play.
8. All penalties given for unsportsmanlike conduct must be reported by the Chair Umpire to the Referee.
9. Subsequent follow-up penalties (suspension, fines, etc.) are not relieved due to point penalties during a tournament.

VIOLATIONS

Verbal abuse of another player, or an official.

Racket abuse, ball abuse, or equipment abuse.

Improper gestures, profanity, or obscenity, either audible or visible.

Failure to resume play within three minutes of an injury or after loss of conditioning.

Intentional delay of the game at any time.

PENALTIES

First Offense	Warning
Second Offense	Point Penalty
Third Offense	Game Penalty
Fourth Offense	Default of Match

LATENESS PENALTIES

Up to 5 minutes	Loss of Toss + 1 game
5 to 10 minutes	Loss of Toss + 2 games
10 to 15 minutes	Loss of Toss + 3 games
Over 15 minutes	Default

CHAPTER 15 EVALUATION

1. Which tournament allows you to play every other player?

2. Which tournament allows you to play "up," but you can be selective of the style of competition you will play against?

3. What tournament is usually selected for tennis teams to determine positions?

4. In weekend tournaments, as well as the U.S. Open, which type of tournament is used?

5. Tournament regulations allow the seeding committee to use a specific ratio for seeding players in the draw. What is that ratio?

6. Where do you place the "byes" on the draw sheet?

7. Losing twice before you are "out" of the tournament indicates a _____ tournament.

8. Name the tournament officials and briefly describe the duties of each.

9. Describe the difference between the Referee and the Umpire.

10. Which official is responsible for keeping a "back-up" score card?

Appendixes

APPENDIX A: RESOURCES

References

Books and Articles

Ashe, Arthur, with Frank Deford. *Arthur Ashe: Portrait in Motion.* Boston: Houghton Mifflin Co.

Barnaby, John. *Advantage Tennis.* Boston: Allyn and Bacon, Inc.

Barnaby, John M. *Advantage Tennis: Racket Work, Tactics, and Logic.* Boston: Allyn and Bacon, Inc.

Brown, Arlene, and Jim Brown. "A Woman's Guide to Beginning Tennis." *The Woman,* 10, No. 2 (June 1975).

Brown, Jim. *Tennis: Teaching, Coaching, and Directing Programs.* Englewood Cliffs, N.J.: Prentice-Hall, Inc.

Brown, Jim. *Tennis Without Lessons.* Englewood Cliffs, N.J.: Prentice-Hall, Inc.

Chamberlain, Brian, and Jim Brown. "Anticipation and the Intermediate Tennis Player," *Athletic Journal,* 51, No. 9 (May 1972).

Gallwey, W. Timothy. *The Inner Game of Tennis.* New York: Random House.

Gensemer, R. E. *Tennis.* Saunders and Co.

Gould, Dick. *Tennis Anyone?* Palo Alto, CA: Mayfield Publishing Company.

Harman, Bob and Keith Monroe. *Use Your Head in Tennis.* New York: Crowell.

Heldman, Julie. "Everything You Want to Know About Equipment," *World Tennis,* 21, No. 1 (June 1973).

Johnson, Joan D. and Paul J. Xanthos. *Tennis.* Dubuque, Iowa: William C. Brown Co.

King, Billie Jean and Kim Chapin. *Tennis to Win.* New York: Harper and Row.

Mason, R. Elaine. *Tennis.* Boston: Allyn and Bacon, Inc.

McPhee, John. *Wimbledon: A Celebration.* New York: The Viking Press.

Murphy, Bill. *Complete Book of Championship Tennis Drills.* West Nyack, N.Y.: Parker Publishing Co., Inc.

Murphy, Chet. *Advanced Tennis.* Dubuque, Iowa: Wm. C. Brown Co.

Murphy, Chet and Bill Murphy. *Tennis for the Player, Teacher and Coach.* Philadelphia: W.B. Saunders Co.

Newcombe, John and Angie with Clarence Mabry. *The Family Tennis Book.* Published by *Tennis* Magazine with Quadrangle. The New York Times Book Co.

Powell, Nick. *The Code.* Princeton, N.J.: United States Lawn Tennis Association.

Ramo, Simon. *Extraordinary Tennis for the Ordinary Player.* New York: Crown Publishers, Inc.

Segura, Pancho, and Gladys Heldman. "Getting in Shape," *World Tennis,* 23, No. 2 (July 1975).

Talbert, Bill with Gordon Greer. *Weekend Tennis.* Garden City, New York: Doubleday and Co., Inc.

Talbert, William and Editors of *Sports Illustrated. The Sports Illustrated Book of Tennis.* Philadelphia: J.B. Lippincott Co.

Tilmanis, Gundars A. *Advanced Tennis for Coaches, Teachers and Players.* Philadelphia: Lea and Febiger.

United States Lawn Tennis Association. *Official Encyclopedia of Tennis.* New York: Harper and Row.

United States Tennis Association. *USTA Official Yearbook.* 51 E. 42nd Street, New York, N.Y., 10017.

Magazines

Tennis Illustrated. Published monthly by the Devonshire Publication Co., 630 Shatto Place, Los Angeles, Ca. 90005.
Tennis Industry. Industry Publishers, Inc., 14961 N.E. 6th Ave., North Miami, FL 33161.
Tennis, Magazine of the Racquet Sports. Official monthly publication of the USPTA. Published by Tennis Features, Inc., 297 Westport Ave., Norwalk, CT 06856.
Tennis. 1255 Portland Place, Boulder, CO 80302.
Tennis World. Royal London House, 171B High Street, Beckenham, Kent, BR3 1BY, England.
World Tennis Magazine. Box 3, Grace Station, New York, N.Y. 10028.

Selected Film List

Anyone for Tennis (color). USTA. 51 East 42nd Street, New York, N.Y. 10017
Beginning Tennis, All-American Productions, PO Box 91, Greeley, CO 80632
Beginning Tennis (color), The Athletic Institute, 805 Merchandise Mart, Chicago, IL 60654
Elementary Fundamentals (BW or Color), All-American Productions, PO Box 91, Greeley, CO 80632
Elementary Tennis (color), 15 min., Dennis Van der Meer, World Tennis, Box 3, Gracie Station, New York, NY 10028
Go for a Winner (color), 37 min., Vic Braden, AMF Head Division, 4801 N. 63rd Street, Boulder, CO 80301
Great Moments in the History of Tennis, American Safety Razor Co., Philip Morris, Inc., 100 Park Avenue, New York, NY 10017.
The Ground Strokes (color), 22 min., Lork and King Associates, Inc., Box 68, Whitfield, IL 60190
Guide to Tennis (color), 22 min., Brentwood Productions, PO Box 49956, Los Angeles, CA 90049
Intermediate and Advanced Tennis (BW), T. N. Rogers Productions, 6641 Clearsprings Road, Santa Susana, CA 93063
Intermediate and Advanced Fundamentals (BW or Color), All-American Productions, PO Box 91, Greeley, CO 80632
Ivan Lendl, Audio Visual Department, USTA Education and Research Center, 729 Alexander Road, Princeton, NJ 08540
Margaret Court Instructional Film (color), 22 min., two units, Scholastic Coach, 50 West 44th Street, New York, NY 10036
1983 *U. S. Open Clay Court Championship,* Audiovisual Department, USTA Education and Research Center, 729 Alexander Road, Princeton, NJ 08540
Playing Better Tennis (color), 25 min., Sport Films and Talents, 7341 Bush Lake Road, Minneapolis, MN 55435
Tennis (color), four parts, 20 min., Forest Hills Productions, Box A619, Madison Square Station, New York, NY 10010
Tennis (color), four units, 20 min. each, AAHPERD Audiovisual Sales, 1201 16th Street N.W., Washington, D.C. 20036
Tennis Class Organization (color), USTA, 51 East 42nd Street, New York, NY 10017
Tennis for Everybody (color), Allegro Film Production, 201 West 52nd Street, New York, NY 10019

218

Tennis, Our Way, Color (150 min.) Arthur Ashe, Vic Braden, Stan Smith, World Vision Home Video, Inc.

Tennis Techniques (color), T. N. Rogers Productions, 6641 Clearsprings Road, Santa Susana, CA 93063

Tennis — Sport of a Lifetime, Part One: Class Organization (color) 30 min., Youth Tennis Foundation of Southern California, 609 West Cahuenga Blvd., Los Angeles, CA 90028

Tennis — Everybody's Game (color), 28 min., Association Films, Inc., 866 Third Avenue, New York, NY 10022

The How-To's of Tennis, Wheaties Sports Federation, Title Insurance Bldg., Minneapolis, MN 55401

Wimbledon 1975-1989 (13 films), Rolex Watch USA, 665 Fifth Ave., NY, NY 10022. Attn: Advertising Dept.

You've Come a Long Way, Baby (color), 25 min., Sports Investors, Inc., 120 East 56th Street, New York, NY 10022

National and Sectional Offices of the United States Tennis Association

National Offices:

United States Tennis Association, Inc., 51 E. 42nd Street, New York, NY 10017 (212) 682-8811

United States Tennis Association Education and Research, 729 Alexander Road, Princeton, NJ 18540 (609) 4552-2580

Sectional Offices:

Caribbean Tennis Association, Box 40439 Manillas Station, Santurce, PR 00940

Eastern Tennis Association, 202 Mamaroneck Avenue, White Plains, NY 10601

Florida Tennis Association, 9620 NE Second Avenue, Room 209, Miami Shores, FL 33138

Hawaii Tennis Association, P. O. Box 411, Honolulu, HI 96809

Intermountain Tennis Association, 1201 S. Parker Road, #102, Denver, CO 80231

Mid-Atlantic Tennis Association, P.O. Drawer F, Springfield, VA 22151

Middle States Tennis Association, 939 Radnor Road, Wayne, PA 19087

Missouri Valley Tennis Association, 722 Walnut, Suite #1, Kansas City, MO 64105

New England Tennis Association, P. O. Box 223, 51 Lincoln Street, Needham, MA 02192

Northern California Tennis Association, 645 Fifty Street, San Francisco, CA 94107

Northwestern Tennis Association, 4608 Drexel Avenue, Edina, MN 55424

Pacific Northwest Tennis Association, 01875 SW Palatine Hill Road, Portland, OR 97219

Southern Tennis Association, 3121 Maple Drive NE, Room 29, Atlanta, GA 30305

Southern California Tennis Association, Los Angeles Tennis Center, P. O. Box 240015, Los Angeles, CA 90024

Southwestern Tennis Association, 3739 S. Siesta, Tempe, AZ 85282

Texas Tennis Association, P. O. Box 192, Austin, TX 78767

Western Tennis Association, 2215 Olympic Street, Springfield, OH 45503

Other Supporting Agencies:

United States Professional Tennis Association, P. O. Box 7077, Wesley Chapel, Florida 34249 (813) 973-3777

United States Tennis Association Membership Services Center, 121 South Service Road, Jerico, NY 11753 (516) 333-7990

APPENDIX B:
NATIONAL TENNIS RATING PROGRAM

Several years ago, the National Tennis Association (NTA), in cooperation with the United States Tennis Association (USTA) and the United States Professional Tennis Association (USPTA), undertook a study of the many tennis rating systems which were proliferating at that time. There were a dozen such systems, in addition to the traditional methods of classification — A, B, C; beginner, advanced beginner, intermediate, etc. With the rapid increase in the number of tennis players regularly participating in programs, a universal rating program was necessary to insure continued satisfaction in the sport.

The consensus of researchers involved in evaluating the existing systems was that to be successful, a rating program had to be universally accepted, and to be universally accepted, it had to be free, easy to administer and non-exclusive.

With this in mind, the NTA, USTA, USPTA, and the IRSA chose to adopt and promote the National Tennis Rating Program (NTRP) to unify the method of classifying players throughout the country. The sponsoring organizations believe that the NTRP is a simple, initial self-placement method of grouping individuals of similar ablity levels and that it allows players to achieve better competition, on-court compatibility, personal challenge, and more enjoyment in the sport.

Rating Categories

1.0-1.9	Beginner	4.0-4.9	Advanced
2.0-2.9	Advanced Beginner	5.0 and up	Tournament and/or Ranked
3.0-3.9	Intermediate		

Your Name _____ Rating _____

Instructor's Comments: _____

_____

_____

_____

Instructor's Rating _____

Instructor's Signature _____

SELF-RATING GUIDELINES

The National Tennis Rating Program provides a simple, initial self-placement method of grouping individuals of similar ability levels for league play, tournaments, group lessons, social competition and club or community programs.

The rating categories are generalizations about skill levels. You may find that you actually play above or below the category which best describes your skill level, depending on your competitive ability. The category you choose is not meant to be permanent, but may be adjusted as your skills change or as your match play demonstrates the need for reclassification. Ultimately your rating is based upon your results in match play.

To place yourself:

A. Begin with 1.0. Read all categories carefully and then decide which one best describes your present ability level.

B. Be certain that you qualify on all points of all preceding categories as well as those in the classification you choose.

C. When rating yourself assume you are playing against a player of the same sex and the same ability.

D. Your self-rating may be verified by a teaching professional, coach, league coordinator or other qualified expert.

E. The person in charge of your tennis program has the right to reclassify you if your self-placement is thought to be inappropriate based upon match results.

NTRP RATING CATEGORIES

1.0 This player is just starting to play tennis.

1.5 This player has limited playing experience and is still working primarily on getting the ball over the net; has some knowledge of scoring but is not familiar with basic positions and procedures for singles and doubles play.

2.0 This player may have had some lessons but needs on-court experience; has obvious stroke weaknesses but is beginning to feel comfortable with singles and doubles play.

2.5 This player has more dependable strokes and is learning to judge where the ball is going; has weak court coverage or is often caught out of position, but is starting to keep the ball in play with other players of the same ability.

3.0 This player can place shots with moderate success; can sustain a rally of slow pace but is not comfortable with all strokes; lacks control when trying for power.

3.5 This player has achieved stroke dependability and direction on shots within reach, including forehand and backhand volleys, but still lacks depth and variety; seldom double faults and occasionally forces errors on the serve.

4.0 This player has dependable strokes on both forehand and backhand sides; has the ability to use a variety of shots including lobs, overheads, approach shots and volleys; can place the first serve and force some errors; is seldom out of position in a doubles game.

4.5 This player has begun to master the use of power and spins; has sound footwork; can control depth of shots and is able to move opponent up and back; can hit first serves with power and accuracy and place the second serve; is able to rush net with some success on serve in singles as well as doubles.

5.0 This player has good shot anticipation; frequently has an outstanding shot or exceptional consistency around which a game may be structured; can regularly hit winners or force errors off of short balls; can successfully execute lobs, drop shots, half volleys and overhead smashes; has good depth and spin on most second serves.

5.5 This player is capable of being ranked at the sectional level, has developed power and/or consistency as a major weapon; can vary strategies and styles of play in a competitive situation.

6.0 This player typically has had intensive training for national tournament competition at the junior and collegiate levels and has obtained a sectional ranking.

6.5 This player has a reasonable chance at succeeding at the 7.0 level, has extensive satellite tournament experience and has obtained a top collegiate ranking.

7.0 This is a world class player, any male currently ranked in the top 500 on the ATP computer and any women ranked in the top 200 on the WTA computer. This player is committed to tournament competition on the international level and whose major source of income is tournament prize winnings.

APPENDIX C: TENNIS SCORE CARD

Directions for Completing Tennis Score Card
(Card is located on the back of these directions.)

1. Fill in information concerning players, event, date, name and school in the space provided.

2. Place the initial of the server (singles or doubles) in the space indicated on the score card under SI (Server's Initials).

3. Place the initials of the players on the right side of the card in the space provided in order to keep an accurate tally of the games won.

4. The check under the column CB is provided as a reminder to change balls if you are using the 9-11 ball change sequence.

5. When scoring points on the card, use a slash "/" diagonally across the small square to indicate which player won.

6. Use the top line always for the server's score in the game being played.

7. At the conclusion of the game, mark the "Game" column appropriately for the player winning the game just concluded. Use "1" then "2," etc., until the set is completed.

8. If a tie-breaker is used when the score is six-all, the bottom of the chart is used, where the "TB" (tie-breaker) is located (below 17). The markings indicate where the service is made (Right or Left), and the letters R and L in the upper and lower squares indicate that the players are serving from opposite sides of the net. The Double Line indicates that the players change sides of the court before serving the next point.

9. At the end of the tiebreaker, the score of 7 is written into the winner's column. The opponent's score ended with 6. Thus the final score of the set is 7-6.

10. When scoring a match, you would be given sufficient scorecards to continue through three sets, if the match lasted that long.

TENNIS SCORE CARD

EVENT_____DATE_____

PLAYERS_____VS_____
         Name   School   Name   School

WON BY _____UMPIRE_____

(At conclusion of match, the umpire must sign the score card and take immediately to official.)

CB		SI	Players change sides after 1st game, 3rd game, etc. POINTS - SET NO. 1																Player Initials Game
	1																		
	2																		
	3																		
	4																		
	5																		
	6																		
	7																		
√	8																		
	9																		
	10																		
	11																		
	12																		
	13																		
	14																		
	15																		
	16																		
	17																		
TB			R			L	R		L	R		L	R		L	R		L	
				L	R			L	R		L	R		L	R				

CB= Change balls; SI= Server's Initials; TB= Tie-breaker; L= Left; R = Right.

Set No. 1   Won by _____ Score _____

APPENDIX D: ERROR CHART

NAME _____

NO-AD SCORING
REG. SCORING

FIRST SET

Game # Server	1st Serve Fault	Serve Returns FHN FHO BHN BHO	Groundstrokes FHN FHO BHN BHO	Volleys NET OUT	Winners US OPP	Aces	Smash NET OUT	Dbl Flt US OPP	Game Won by
1									
2									
3									
4									
5									
6									
7									
8									
9									
10									
11									
12									
TB									

KEY: **FHN** = FOREHAND INTO NET, **FHO** = FOREHAND OUT. **BHN** = BACKHAND INTO NET. BHO = BACKHAND OUT
Use a "✔" to indicate your mark in the appropriate column.

NAME _____

ERROR CHART

NO-AD SCORING
REG. SCORING

SECOND SET

Game #	Server	1st Serve Fault	Serve Returns				Groundstrokes				Volleys		Winners		Aces	Smash		Dbl Flt		Game
			FHN	FHO	BHN	BHO	FHN	FHO	BHN	BHO	NET	OUT	US	OPP		NET	OUT	US	OPP	Won by
1																				
2																				
3																				
4																				
5																				
6																				
7																				
8																				
9																				
10																				
11																				
12																				
TB																				

KEY: **FHN** = FOREHAND INTO NET, **FHO** = FOREHAND OUT, **BHN** = BACKHAND INTO NET, BHO = BACKHAND OUT
Use a "✓" to indicate your mark in the appropriate column.

ERROR CHART

NO-AD SCORING
REG. SCORING

NAME _____

THIRD SET

Game # Server	1st Serve Fault	Serve Returns FHN FHO BHN BHO	Groundstrokes FHN FHO BHN BHO	Volleys NET OUT	Winners US OPP	Aces	Smash NET OUT	Dbl Flt US OPP	Game Won by
1									
2									
3									
4									
5									
6									
7									
8									
9									
10									
11									
12									
TB									

KEY: **FHN** = FOREHAND INTO NET, **FHO** = FOREHAND OUT. **BHN** = BACKHAND INTO NET. BHO = BACKHAND OUT
Use a "✓" to indicate your mark in the appropriate column.

Match Won By: _____   Score: _____

APPENDIX E: TENNIS EXAMINATION

True-False Questions

1. There is evidence that a tennis-like game has been played for over 10,000 years.

2. "Jeu de paume" is another name for hitting a stuffed object over a rope with the bare hand.

3. Mary Outerbridge, while vacationing in Bermuda, learned the game of tennis and brought it to the U.S. in 1874.

4. The U.S. Championships have always been held in New York at either Forest Hills or the new tennis stadium at Flushing Meadows.

5. The Grand Slam of Tennis means that the player, male or female, has won the championships of the United States, England, France and Austria.

6. Competition between the U.S. and England, for women only, is called the Wightman Cup Championships.

7. Light tennis rackets, when compared to medium weights, are around 13-14 ounces.

8. Racket presses, while used frequently with the older wood models, are seldom used with the newer metal and composite frames.

9. There are no limitations to length and width of the frames of modern tennis rackets, according to the rules.

10. Tennis courts should be oriented on a North to South line.

11. A score of deuce indicates that both players have won at least two points each and both have the same score.

12. The twelve-point tie-breaker is the most popular one used today.

13. In the twelve-point breaker, the service order in doubles follows the same pattern as that of the normal service rotation.

14. As server, I have won two points to my opponent's three. The score in this game is 40-30.

15. In a pro set the winner must be two games ahead of the opponent.

16. My partner served the last game of the previous set, which we won. It is now my responsibility to serve the first game for our team, when our turn comes up again.

17. It is considered poor sportsmanship to stroke a ball directly at the opponent during a play.

18. When using the VASSS scoring system, the winner of the game must be two points ahead to win the game.

19. The term "shake hands grip" refers to the continental grip.

20. The western grip is recommended for beginners since it alters the face of the racket causing the ball to rise to an upward trajectory that will take it over the net.

21. The primary goal of a beginner should be to develop control.

22. These words — control, speed, spin, accuracy and power — are ranked in the correct order.

23. From 50 to 70 percent of your success in tennis will be directly attributed to successful footwork.

24. The reverse pivot is used when the ball is coming in close to the body.

25. The contact point when hitting a forehand is right in front of the "belt buckle," and a comfortable reach from the body.

26. At the completion of the forehand stroke, the weight is almost totally on the forward foot closest to the net.

27. The best server should serve first when you and your partner play doubles.

28. The volley is used when the player is on the attack.

29. A good backswing should be used when hitting a volley, as it allows great power and speed on the stroke.

30. When receiving serve in doubles, you should attempt to drop the return right at the feet of the incoming server.

31. The basic serve for most players is the flat serve.

32. The toss for the twist serve is slightly more over the head and to the rear of the player when compared with the slice and the flat serves.

33. The toughest serve to master is the cannonball, or flat serve.

34. The parallel theory in doubles means that the players strive to position themselves parallel to the net whenever possible.

35. The formation for "Australian doubles" is seldom used in good competition.

36. Canadian doubles uses three players, for a total of six per court.

37. In good doubles play, most serves should go to the opponents' backhand side.

38. Poaching is a term used in doubles to describe a situation where both players end up covering the same side of the court.

39. A half-volley is a stroke whereby the racket contacts the ball just as it rebounds from the court, very near the ground.

40. As a general rule, most tennis players do not warm up properly.

41. A player is serving in a singles game. The serve hits the net post and then hits the court in the proper service area. The serve should be ruled a let serve.

42. I go to the net for an overhand smash but lose the ball in the sun. The ball glances off my shoulder but I lob it back across the net on first bounce. I lost the point when it hit me.

43. A serve is not a fault if the server decides not to strike it and catches the ball instead.

44. The score is 15 all. The server by mistake serves from the left-hand court. She wins the point. She then serves again from the right-hand court, delivering a fault. The mistake is then discovered. The last point stands.

45. The next service should be from the right-hand court, and the server has served one fault.

46. If a receiver claims to be not ready and does not make an effort to return a second service, the server may not claim the point even though the service was good.

47. One player hits a clear winning overhead smash but in the process ruptures the ball causing a loss in compression. The point should be allowed because he hit a clear winner.

48. In doubles competition one player does not appear in time to play. The remaining player claims that the rules allow him to compete against the opposing team.

When at the net in doubles with your partner hitting from the backcourt:

49. Hold your position at the net regardless of your partner's position.

50. Move toward your partner when you see an opening developing between you two.

51. Hold your position at the net when your partner lobs.

52. On volleys the left hand is used to help move the racket during the backswing.

53. On volleys a crossover step provides maximum reach for wide shots.

54. Most tennis players do not warm up properly before a match.

55. A good axiom to follow is "play every point and give nothing away."

56. It is illegal to serve underhand in tennis.

Serves that are consistently misdirected to the left can be corrected by:

57. Placing the racket more toward the nose of the imaginary face on the ball.

58. Tossing the ball farther in front (toward the net).

59. Changing your stance to make your body face more to the right.

60. Making your swing resemble that of the American twist serve.

The receiver in singles:

61. Should use his or her most consistent shots on all crucial points.

62. Should try always to place the return deep to the server's backhand.

63. Should stand on an imaginary line that bisects the server's angles.

64. Should drive every return, especially against high-bouncing spin serves.

65. Should always stand back far enough to have time for a full swing and a full-speed shot.

66. Should sometimes hit crosscourt, though that placement may be to the opponent's stronger stroke.

67. Can often minimize the effectiveness of the server's first volley by hitting directly at the server.

Recommended uses for the chop/slice ground stroke are:

68. To return a high-bouncing spin serve.

69. As an approach shot during a rally.

70. As a defensive shot when you have been forced wide.

71. As a half-volley when coming in to the net.

72. When swinging late on a deeply hit, high bounce shot.

73. The volley is usually made from the back-court area.

74. Whenever possible, the head of the racket should be below the handle when making a volley.

75. Good lobbing is more essential in dislodging opponents from the net in doubles than the opponent in singles.

76. When your opponent raises his or her racket head higher than the handle just before hitting, you know the ball will have backspin.

77. A drop shot is a good return shot against a drop shot.

78. If losing a match try to slow the play to get yourself together.

79. In most doubles teams you will find the person with the strongest backhand in the add court.

80. If clearly out-classed, go to a reckless chance-taking type of play.

Completion:

81. In the two-handed backhand, the reach limitations can be overcome with proper emphasis on _____.

82. To most people, the _____ is the most difficult stroke in tennis.

83. In a tennis match approximately _____ percent of points are errors.

234

84. Keeping the ball in the backcourt and forcing the opponent to stay behind the baseline utilizes the _____theory of play.

85. In Australian doubles, the partner of the server stands in front of the _____.

86. The first server in doubles should be the _____ server.

87. _____is used by the net player to cut off the service return.

88. A _____is an illegal shot causing the ball to be slung or hit twice before crossing the net.

89. To win the game served by the opponent is to _____serve.

90. A _____is a lightly hit ball having backspin which barely clears the net.

Work out this problem.

A & B are playing X & Y. A and X are the first servers. A serves first from the North court. X receives backhand as does B. Six games have been played. The team serving now has won four of the games and is ahead in this game having won three points to one. Answer these questions:

91. _____ is the team now serving (team).

92. _____ is the server (player).

93. _____ is the receiver (player).

94. _____ is the side (North or South) being served from.

95. _____ is the receiving court for this point.

96. _____ has four games.

97. _____ has three points.

98. _____ is the next server.

99. _____ is the side (N or S) being served from (next game).

100. _____ is playing net for the server, now.

APPENDIX F: CLASSIC EXCUSES

Tennis players are like people who fish— they always have an excuse for letting the "big one" get off the hook. As you become a more experienced player you will hear and use some of the classic excuses listed below. These are the ones the authors have heard most frequently over a lifetime of play.

I just couldn't move out there.
The sun really bothered my game.
Nothing went right.
He/She hit every line.
My elbow was really hurting.
My knee hurt.
I have blisters on my feet.
I have a sore wrist.
I just couldn't get going.
I couldn't keep the ball in.
My serve wasn't working.
My hand kept slipping on the grip.
I broke a string.
My racket was just re-strung.
My racket is too loose/tight.
I ran out of gas.
He/She just hits junk shots.
He/She had an easier first round.
My timing was off.
It was too windy to play well.
I was using a borrowed racket.
I didn't have much time to practice.
I never play well on hard courts.
I drew a sandbagger.
I left my glasses at home.
I had a bad day.
The balls were dead.
The courts were in terrible shape.
The net was too high.
He/She has a court in his back yard.
I'm not used to clay.
The lights were awful.

I ate too much lunch.
I drew a seeded player.
I had to play a match this morning.
I had a bad draw.
I just choked.
He/She was just too quick for me.
I hate to play a pusher.
He/She cheated.
I lost my "cool."
I didn't have time to warm up.
I was praying for rain.
I'm glad I didn't get hurt.
I know how to play him/her now.
Next time it won't even be close.
I just changed rackets; I haven't adjusted yet.
I forgot my hat.
The sun was in my eyes all during the match.
The umpire liked him/her better.
I'm not used to those balls.
His/her mother kept screaming during the match.
The spectators really got to me.
The girl in the bikini got to me.
There wasn't any water around anywhere.
The players on the next court made too much noise.
The airplanes overhead really distracted me.
His/Her "grunts" really upset my concentration.

We earnestly hope that you do not have to resort to our "list." May you always be a "winner!"

APPENDIX G: TENNIS PLAYERS

As with any book, there comes a time when authors "run out of words." And so it is with us. As you continue to play the game you will begin to recognize this next group of "players." So with tongue in cheek, we close this book with a few descriptions of players we have known. And who knows? In time you may even resemble one of them.

First there is the "Crafty Clarence" type. This person is usually older, highly intelligent, and knows every trick in the book for taking points the easy way. This includes talking you out of them. He practices gamesmanship to the nth degree. He rarely looks like a good tennis player, but somehow always does just enough to beat you. His opponents usually stomp away shaking their heads and muttering to themselves, "How did I lose to that guy?" *Advice:* Beware of this person, for even if you win you will not know why, plus you will feel as though you did all the running. And you probably did.

Crafty Clarence

How about "Apologetic Alice"? This type of player is forever apologizing. If she rips an ace by you, she says, "I'm sorry," or if she hits the line she says she is "sorry." After about the third or fourth "I'm sorry" you know she is not sorry or she would ease up on you. What she is doing is apologizing because you are so bad, and she has to play with you. Of course, this just makes you feel worse. *Advice:* Tell her she doesn't have to apologize to you for making a good shot—only if she loses the match!

Apologetic Alice

Then there is "Stylish Stella." Stella may not stand out as a tennis player, but she works hard at being noticed. She rarely sweats because that would ruin her outfit, makeup, or hairdo. However, she can always be counted on to model the latest tennis attire and she would rather be caught dead than to wear the same outfit twice in one week. Usually an infrequent court player, she spends a lot of time on the club porch or

Stylish Stella

238

some other conspicuous spot where she can be seen. *Advice:* If you are a married male, avoid this type like the plague. If you are a married female with a tennis-playing husband, watch her like a hawk.

Have you ever played with a "Reckless Ralph" type? This guy always goes for the "big one." He is a gambler of the highest order, usually preferring to serve and volley since that is more spectacular and he can lose more quickly. Losing doesn't seem to bother Ralph, however, probably because he does it so often. *Advice:* Smile when you draw Ralph as an opponent. Run in the opposite direction when he wants to team up with you.

Reckless Ralph

Do you remember old "Drop Shot Charley"? This player usually chops and hacks his way through every shot. He is usually an old guy who has been playing so long he has barnacles on his racket. He invariably plays the baseline and is tough as nails. *Advice:* Drop shot him before he drop shots you and watch out for his lob. Drop Shot Charleys are often sadists at heart and nothing pleases them more than to make you run to the net and then back to the baseline for an entire match.

Drop Shot Charley

"Practice Paul" is another dear old character found at any tennis club. This guy spends more time practicing than playing. He is always taking lessons, is always hitting against the board, or practicing serves, but never seems to get any better. *Advice:* These guys are usually beautiful people. Humor them by teaming up as often as possible, and don't forget to pass out the compliments whenever you can.

Practice Paul

Another fairly common type is what we jokingly refer to as the "Smiling Sam" personality. This person shows you his teeth at all times. His face is in a constant grin or grimace. Of course, it may be you are running him so hard that he has to breathe with his mouth open and he could have adenoids. Or he could just be a nice guy who doesn't take his tennis that seriously. *Advice:* If it's a breathing problem he should "run out of gas." If it's a grimace, you are in for a long day, because he is dead serious.

Who could forget the "Hurting Henry" type of character? The Hurting Henrys are generally middle-aged guys who limp around on the court like they are about to fall over. The disconcerting thing is they always seem to get your best shot, and are able to turn it on when they have to. During the exchange of courts they will always tell you why they are limping, and ask you to take it easy on them. If they are older than you they will always tell you how much older they are than you. *Advice:* Watch these guys. They are usually tough, tough, tough, even though they may have age and lack conditioning. Since they use this as a stalling device, speed up the play whenever possible. Also, be careful about feeling sorry for them.

Who hasn't played a "Forgetful Frank"? This character always seems to forget the score when you are ahead or on some very crucial point. They also forget the game score. *Advice:* Since these people always make mistakes in their favor they are usually hard to beat and you must remind them of the score as often as possible. Particularly when you are serving and on odd numbered games when changing courts.

How about "Big Foot Fred"? Fred is not noticed much on hard courts, except that he frequently falls down or into the net. But on rubico or clay courts he is an absolute terror. When he finishes playing the court looks as though a herd of elephants has wandered through. He

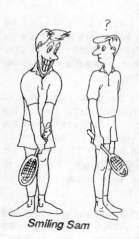

Smiling Sam

Forgetful Frank

Hurting Henry

Big Foot Fred

does leave his mark on any court he plays on. *Advice:* There is no hope for Big Footed Freds. Either try to play before they do or ask for a court other than the one they used.

Then there is the "Killer Kane" type of player. This type of player begins the game with a glint in their eye. They feel they must hit you with the ball to make their day. *Advice:* This type is dangerous to your health, but easy to beat because they usually have an uncontrollable temper.

"Timid Tilly" is generally young and doesn't really know why she is playing tennis but it seems to be the "in thing." She wouldn't think of swinging hard at the ball because she might hurt it or the persons feelings she is playing with. She usually just bumps the ball with little follow through and no backswing. *Advice:* A Tilly does not usually stay long with tennis, so be patient with them.

We can't forget "Temperamental Tom." Tom screams, cusses, and talks out loud. What you never know is whether he is screaming or cussing at you. These guys also are known to throw rackets, hit balls at opponents, hit balls over fences, hit themselves with their racket and to generally behave like an ass. *Advice:* Smile, thus making them more angry. Then they are really easy to beat. If he is your partner, find somebody else.

Have you ever played against a "Screamin' Steven" type? This guy was once a football or karate player and was taught to exhale or grunt forcefully with every hit. He therefore chases around the court grunting on every forehand and backhand. When he gets the overhead, high volley or serve, then he really goes wild. Advice: This kind of player can get to you psychologically if you let them. If they have a glint in their eye

Killer Kane

Timid Tilly

Temperamental Tom

Screamin' Steven

along with a grunt they usually like to hit people with the tennis ball. Watch them closely but laugh at them at every opportunity. If you can "hang-in" they will usually crack.

In doubles play there is always a "Harold the Hog" type. Harold believes he must hit at least three fourths of all shots, so proceeds to force his partner off the court. He is the take charge type, freely gives advice, and will tell everyone exactly why they won or lost. *Advice:* If you don't mind hitting only 25% of the shots and you are winning with him then by all means retain this person as a partner. If you wish to discourage him try grunting a few pig-like "oinks" when he steals one of your shots. You might also deliberately hit him with your racket and then say "I am terribly sorry, but it really was my shot you know."

Harold the Hog

"Spacey Stacey" never knows the score or whose serve it is. As a matter of fact, she generally knows very little about anything. She just wanders around on the court and must be told what to do and when to do it. She is a delight to play with, if you don't care whether you win or lose. *Advice:* It takes a certain kind of personality to play with Stacey and you had better have it or you will climb the wall.

Spacey Stacey

Who can forget "Lesson Larry"? The nice thing about playing against or with Larry is you always get a free tennis lesson, whether you want it or not. He always knows exactly what is wrong with all your shots. *Advice:* Unless he is an experienced player and teacher, you should run when you see him coming. This guy can really louse up your game and your mind. On the other hand, if he knows what he is doing he can be very helpful, and provide an inexpensive way to learn the game. However, a word of

Lesson Larry

caution. Knowledgeable and good players who can teach, are hard to find.

No one can play tennis very long without running into a character which I refer to as "Grim Jim." The "Grim Jims" regard a tennis match in the same manner as going into military combat. From the time they step on the court until the time they walk off they do not smile, they do not exchange pleasantries, they say little or nothing. It is though everything is being held in as the pressure builds. *Advice:* If you play tennis as a social, gregarious person you will not have much fun with these characters. As a matter of fact you will probably feel quite uncomfortable. Since they do not hold their feelings in they will sometimes blow sky high if you can trigger the right button. If you want to win, the secret is finding what bothers them the most and then doing it.

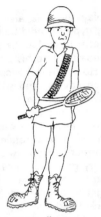

Grim Jim

Probably the person who enjoys his tennis the most is old "Guzzling Gus." Now Gus doesn't play tennis for any reason except as an excuse to drink. He is out to have a good time drinking and wants to obtain a little exercise along with his primary pastime. *Advice:* The best way to spot "Gus" is by looking for a cooler or jug. They usually are fun to play with if you don't much care whether you win or lose. They invariably play better after one or two drinks and the longer they play (and drink) the worse they play. However, they usually laugh more and worry less about their mistakes so it all balances out. Be careful about betting with these guys. Some can give academy award performances.

Guzzling Gus

Another public court fixture is "Country Boy Bill." The distinguishing feature about Bill is that he always tries to look the part. He arrives at the court with never more than one racket, which is usually a battered antique. He wears baggy shorts, and frequently a stained baseball cap that is at least 10 years old. If he plays on a hard surface he usually wears an old pair of basketball shoes. If he wins, which he usually does, he invariably hangs his head and mumbles "Aw shucks, I was lucky today." *Advice:* Beware of this type; they will either be really bad or extremely tough, but rarely in between. They also have a tendency toward being unorthodox.

Country Boy Bill

How about that old character "Moonball Mickey"? Moonball will invariably amble on to the court with two or three towels and a jug of something. He always wears a hat or cap and usually wears a head band and wristlets. You see he knows it is going to be a long match and is prepared for it. These guys rarely weigh more than 160 pounds of pure leather and are as tough as nails. Their motto is "If I keep the ball in play long enough you will make the mistake, not me." They specialize in big rackets and heavy tennis balls. *Advice:* If you are going to overpower one of these people you had better be a much better player. Otherwise get ready for a long day. Also, try to play either early or late in the day so they cannot use the sun and wind against you. They play every percentage. Since they rarely hit the ball hard you must take the game to them and try to force them into a different style. Also be prepared for a sore neck from looking up so much.

Moonball Mickey

"Professional Pauls" are perhaps the easiest to spot of all. They always carry 2-4 rackets on the court before every match. "Professional Pauls" want their opponents to think they are very good, and they will do everything possible to play the part. They dress like a hot shot tennis player even if they lack the ability. They also tend to have more tennis knowledge than ability. *Advice:* If you see your match opponent coming

Professional Paul

to the court with an armful of rackets you can bet he is pretty good or pretty bad. If he lacks a good tan you may have a chance.

Whoops, we almost forgot "Charging Chester." Chester was a Marine in his younger days and believes the only way to beat someone is to "take it to em," which he does at every opportunity. He even invents opportunities like when he hits a short ball to an opponent's forehand. Aggression is his middle name. *Advice:* This guy can be dangerous to your health if he is your doubles partner or you are hitting short overheads. If he is your opponent, you should be smiling.

Charging Chester

Last but not least we have old "Baseline Bill." Now old Bill has played tennis since he was knee high to a pup and knows every trick in the book. He usually is a weather-beaten old codger who will do anything except come to the net or hit an overhead. He prefers to let you make the mistakes while jerking you from corner to corner. *Advice:* Make him run before he can do it to you. Also, by any means possible bring him to the net.

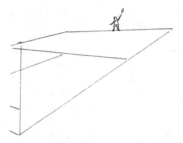

Baseline Bill

In closing, remember that tennis is a fun game. If you can look for the lighter side (acknowledgeably hard to do at times) you will last a lot longer and develop a healthier outlook on life. Also, it helps to be able to laugh at yourself since it tempers the psychological and physiological pain of growing older — and losing more.

APPENDIX H:
UNABRIDGED RULES OF TENNIS

The Rules of Tennis are reprinted with the permission of the United States Tennis Association. Rules are amended annually; the following are the latest available at press time. Individual copies of the rules may be purchased from the USTA Educational and Research Center, Publications Department, 729 Alexander Road, Princeton, NJ 08540.

Contents of Rules

Rules of Tennis

Explanatory Note

The following Rules and Cases and Decisions are the official Code of the International Tennis Federation, of which the United States Tennis Association is a member. USTA Comments have the same weight and force in USTA tournaments as do ITF Cases and Decisions.

When a match is played without officials the principles and guidelines set forth in the USTA Publication, The Code, shall apply in any situation not covered by the rules.

Except where otherwise stated, every reference in these Rules to the masculine includes the feminine gender.

A vertical line in the margin by a rule indicates a change made by the ITF in September 1989 and which took effect January 1, 1990. A vertical line by a USTA Comment indicates a change made since the last edition.

The Singles Game

RULE 1

The Court

The court shall be a rectangle 78 feet (23.77m.) long and 27 feet (8.23m.) wide. **USTA Comment:** See Rule 34 for a doubles court.

It shall be divided across the middle by a net suspended from a cord or metal cable of a maximum diameter of one-third of an inch (0.8cm.), the ends of which shall be attached to, or pass over, the tops of two posts, which shall be not more than 6 inches (15cm.) square or 6 inches (15cm.) in diameter. These posts shall not be higher than 1 inch (2.5 cm.) above the top of the net cord. The centres of the posts shall be 3 feet (0.914m.) outside the court on each side and the height of the posts shall be such that the top of the cord or metal cable shall be 3 feet 6 inches (1.07m.) above the ground.

When a combined doubles (see Rule 34) and singles court with a doubles net is used for singles, the net must be supported to a height of 3 feet 6 inches (1.07m.) by means of two posts, called "singles sticks", which shall be not more than 3 inches (7.5cm.) square or 3 inches (7.5cm.) in diameter. The centres of the singles sticks shall be 3 feet (0.914m.) outside the singles court on each side.

The net shall be extended fully so that it fills completely the space between the two posts and shall be of sufficiently small mesh to prevent the ball passing through. The height of the net shall be 3 feet (0.914m.) at the centre, where it shall be held down taut by a strap not more than 2 inches (5cm.) wide and completely white in colour. There shall be a band covering the cord or metal cable and the top of the net of not less than 2 inches (5cm.) nor more than 2½ inches (6.3cm.) in depth on each side and completely white in colour.

There shall be no advertisement on the net, strap, band or singles sticks.

The lines bounding the ends and sides of the Court shall respectively be called the base-lines and the side-lines. On each side of the net, at a distance of 21 feet (6.40m.) from it and parallel with it, shall be drawn the service-lines. The space on each side of the net between the service-line and the side-lines shall be divided into two equal parts called the service-courts by the centre service-line, which must be 2 inches (5cm.) in width, drawn half-way between, and parallel with, the side-lines. Each base-line shall be bisected by an imaginary continuation of the centre service-line to a line 4 inches (10cm.) in length and 2 inches (5cm.) in width called the centre mark drawn inside the Court, at right angles to and in contact with such base-lines. All other lines shall be not less than 1 inch (2.5cm.) nor more than 2 inches (5cm.) in width, except the base-line, which may be 4 inches (10cm.) in width, and all measurements shall be made to the outside of the lines. All lines shall be of uniform colour.

If advertising or any other material is placed at the back of the court, it may not contain white, or yellow. A light colour may only be used if this does not interfere with the vision of the players.

If advertisements are placed on the chairs of the Linesmen sitting at the back of the court, they may not contain white, or yellow. A light colour may only be used if this does not interfere with the vision of the players.

Note: In the case of the *Davis Cup* or other Official Championships of the International Tennis Federation, there shall be a space behind each base-line of not less than 21 feet (6.4m.), and at the sides of not less than 12 feet (3.66m.). The chairs of the linesmen may be placed at the back of the court within the 21 feet or at the side of the court within the 12 feet, provided they do not protrude into that area more than 3 feet (.914m).

USTA Comment: *An approved method for obtaining proper net tautness is this: Loosen the center strap; tighten the net cord until it is approximately 40 inches above the ground, being careful not to overtighten the net; tighten the center strap until the center of the net is 36 inches above the ground. These measurements should always be made before the first match of the day. For a plan of the court see the preceding diagram.*

RULE 2
Permanent Fixtures

The permanent fixtures of the Court shall include not only the net, posts, singles sticks, cord or metal cable, strap and band, but also, where there are any such, the back and side stops, the stands, fixed or movable seats and chairs round the Court, and their occupants, all other fixtures around and above the Court, and the Umpire, Net-cord Judge, Foot-fault Judge, Linesmen and Ball Boys when in their respective places.

Note: For the purpose of this Rule, the word "Umpire" comprehends the Umpire, the persons entitled to a seat on the Court, and all those persons designated to assist the Umpire in the conduct of a match.

RULE 3
The Ball

The ball shall have a uniform outer surface and shall be white or yellow in colour. If there are any seams, they shall be stitchless.

The ball shall be more than two and a half inches (6.35cm.) and less than two and five-eighths inches (6.67cm.) in diameter, and more than two ounces (56.7 grams) and less than two and one-sixteenth ounces (58.5 grams) in weight.

The ball shall have a bound of more than 53 inches (135cm.) and less than 58 inches (147cm.) when dropped 100 inches (254cm.) upon a concrete base.

The ball shall have a forward deformation of more than .220 of an inch (.56cm.) and less than .290 of an inch (.74cm.) and a return deformation of more than .350 of an inch (.89cm.) and less than .425 of an inch (1.08cm.) at 18 lb. (8.165kg.) load. The two deformation figures shall be the averages of three individual readings along three axes of the ball and no two individual readings shall differ by more than .030 of an inch (.08cm.) in each case.

For play above 4,000 feet (1219m) in altitude above sea level, two additional types of ball may be used. The first type is identical to those described above except that the bound shall be more than 48 inches (121.92cm) and less than 53 inches (135cm) and the ball shall have an internal pressure that is greater than the external pressure. This type of tennis ball is commonly known as a pressurized ball. The second type is identical to those described above except that they shall have a bound of more than 53 inches (135cm) and less than 58 inches (147cm) and shall have an internal pressure that is approximately equal to the external pressure and have been acclimatized for 60 days or more at the altitude of the specific tournament. This type of tennis ball is commonly known as a zero-pressure or non-pressurized ball.

All tests for bound, size and deformation shall be made in accordance with the Regulations in the Appendix hereto.

RULE 4

The Racket

Rackets failing to comply with the following specifications are not approved for play under the Rules of Tennis:

(a) The hitting surface of the racket shall be flat and consist of a pattern of crossed strings connected to a frame and alternately interlaced or bonded where they cross; and the stringing pattern shall be generally uniform, and in particular not less dense in the centre than in any other area. The strings shall be free of attached objects and protrusions other than those utilized solely and specifically to limit or prevent wear and tear or vibration and which are reasonable in size and placement for such purposes.

(b) The frame of the racket shall not exceed 32 inches (81.28cm.) in overall length, including the handle and 12½ inches (31.75cm.) in overall width. The strung surface shall not exceed 15½ inches (39.37cm.) in overall length, and 11½ inches (29.21cm.) in overall width.

(c) The frame, including the handle, shall be free of attached objects and devices other than those utilized solely and specifically to limit or prevent wear and tear or vibration, or to distribute weight. Any objects and devices must be reasonable in size and placement for such purposes.

(d) The frame, including the handle and the strings, shall be free of any device which makes it possible to change materially the shape of the racket, or to change the weight distribution, during the playing of a point.

The International Tennis Federation shall rule on the question of whether any racket or prototype complies with the above specifications or is otherwise approved, or not approved, for play. Such ruling may be undertaken on its own initiative, or upon application by any party with a bona fide interest therein, including any player, equipment manufacturer or National Association or members thereof. Such rulings and applications shall be made in accordance with the applicable Review and Hearing Procedures of the International Tennis Federation, copies of which may be obtained from the office of the Secretary.

Case 1. Can there be more than one set of strings on the hitting surface of a racket?
Decision. No. The rule clearly mentions a pattern, and not patterns, of crossed strings.
Case 2. Is the stringing pattern of a racket considered to be generally uniform and flat if the strings are on more than one plane?
Decision. No.
Case 3. Can a vibration dampening device be placed on the strings of a racket and if so, where can it be placed?
Decision. Yes; but such devices may only be placed outside the pattern of crossed strings.

RULE 5
Server and Receiver
The players shall stand on opposite sides of the net; the player who first delivers the ball shall be called the Server, and the other the Receiver.

Case 1. Does a player, attempting a stroke, lose the point if he crosses an imaginary line in the extension of the net,
(a) before striking the ball,
(b) after striking the ball?
Decision. He does not lose the point in either case by crossing the imaginary line and provided he does not enter the lines bounding his opponent's Court (Rule 20 (e)). In regard to hindrance, his opponent may ask for the decision of the Umpire under Rules 21 and 25.
Case 2. The Server claims that the Receiver must stand within the lines bounding his Court. Is this necessary?
Decision. No. The Receiver may stand wherever he pleases on his own side of the net.

RULE 6
Choice of Ends and Service
The choice of ends and the right to be Server or Receiver in the first game shall be decided by toss. The player winning the toss may choose or require his opponent to choose:

(a) The right to be Server or Receiver, in which case the other player shall choose the end; or

(b) The end, in which case the other player shall choose the right to be Server or Receiver.

USTA Comment: *These choices should be made promptly after the toss and are irrevocable, except that if the match is postponed or suspended before the start of the match. See Case 1 below.*

Case 1. Do players have the right to new choices if the match is postponed or suspended before it has started?
Decision. Yes. The toss stands, but new choices may be made with respect to service and end.

RULE 7
The Service
The service shall be delivered in the following manner. Immediately before commencing to serve, the Server shall stand with both feet at rest behind (i.e. further from the net than) the base-line, and within the imaginary continuations of the centre-mark and side-line. The Server shall then project the ball by hand into the air in any direction and before it hits the ground strike it with his racket, and the delivery shall be deemed to have been completed at the moment of the impact of the racket and the ball. A player with the use of only one arm may utilize his racket for the projection.

USTA Comment: *The service begins when the Server takes a ready position* | *(i.e., both feet at rest behind the baseline) and ends when his racket makes contact with the ball, or when he misses the ball in attempting to serve it.*

Case 1. May the Server in a singles game take his stand behind the portion of the base-line between the side-lines of the Singles Court and the Doubles Court?
Decision. No.

USTA Comment: *The server may stand anywhere in back of the baseline between the imaginary extensions of the center mark and the singles sideline.*

Case 2. If a player, when serving, throws up two or more balls instead of one, does he lose that service?
Decision. No. A let should be called, but if the Umpire regards the action as deliberate he may take action under Rule 21.

| **USTA Comment:** *There is no restriction regarding the kind of service which may be used; that is, the player may use an underhand or overhand service at his discretion.*

RULE 8

Foot Fault

(a) The Server shall throughout the delivery of the service:

(i) Not change his position by walking or running. The Server shall not by slight movements of the feet which do not materially affect the location originally taken up by him, be deemed "to change his position by walking or running".

(ii) Not touch, with either foot, any area other than that behind the base-line within the imaginary extensions of the centre mark and side-lines.

(b) The word "foot" means the extremity of the leg below the ankle.

USTA Comment: *This rule covers the most decisive stroke in the game, and there is no justification for its not being obeyed by players and enforced by officials. No official has the right to instruct any umpire to disregard violations of it. In a non-officiated match, the Receiver, or his partner, may call foot faults after all efforts (appeal to the server, request for an umpire, etc.) have failed and the foot faulting is so flagrant as to be clearly perceptible from the Receiver's side.*

It is improper for any official to warn a player that he is in danger of having a foot fault called on him. On the other hand, if a player, in all sincerity, asks for an explanation of how he foot faulted, either the Line Umpire or the Chair Umpire should give him that information.

RULE 9

Delivery of Service

(a) In delivering the service, the Server shall stand alternately behind the right and left Courts beginning from the right in every game. If service from a wrong half of the Court occurs and is undetected, all play resulting from such wrong service or services shall stand, but the inaccuracy of station shall be corrected immediately it is discovered.

(b) The ball served shall pass over the net and hit the ground within the Service Court which is diagonally opposite, or upon any line bounding such Court, before the Receiver returns it.

USTA Comment: *See Rule 18.*

Service Fault

The Service is a fault:

(a) If the Server commits any breach of Rules 7, 8 or 9(b);

(b) If he misses the ball in attempting to strike it;

(c) If the ball served touches a peramanent fixture (other than the net, strap or band) before it hits the ground.

Case 1. After throwing a ball up preparatory to serving, the Server decides not to strike at it and catches it instead. Is it a fault?

Decision. No. **USTA Comment:** As long as the Server makes no attempt to strike the ball, it is immaterial whether he catches it in his hand or on his racket or lets it drop to the ground.

Case 2. In serving in a singles game played on a Doubles Court with doubles posts and singles sticks, the ball hits a singles stick and then hits the ground within the lines of the correct Service Court. Is this a fault or a let?

Decision. In serving it is a fault, because the singles stick, the doubles post, and that portion of the net, or band between them are permanent fixtures. (Rules 2 and 10, and note to Rule 24.).

USTA Comment: *The significant point governing Case 2 is that the part of the net and band "outside" the singles sticks is not part of the net over which this singles match is being played. Thus such a serve is a fault under the provisions of Article (c) above . . . By the same token, this would be a fault also if it were a singles game played with permanent posts in the singles position. (See Case 1 under Rule 24 for difference between "service" and "good return" with respect to a ball's hitting a net post.)*

USTA Comment: *In a non-officiated singles match, each player makes calls for all balls landing on, or aimed at, his side of the net. In doubles, normally the Receiver's partner makes the calls with respect to the service line, with the Receiver calling the side and center lines, but either partner may make the call on any ball he clearly sees out.*

RULE 11

Second Service

After a fault (if it is the first fault) the Server shall serve again from behind the same half of the Court from which he served that fault, unless the service was from the wrong half, when, in accordance with Rule 9, the Server shall be entitled to one service only from behind the other half.

Case 1. A player serves from a wrong Court. He loses the point and then claims it was a fault because of his wrong station.

Decision. The point stands as played and the next service should be from the correct station according to the score.

Case 2. The point score being 15 all, the Server, by mistake, serves from the left-hand Court. He wins the point. He then serves again from the right-hand Court, delivering a fault. This mistake in station is then discovered. Is he entitled to the previous point? From which Court should he next serve?

Decision. The previous point stands. The next service should be from the left-hand Court, the score being 30/15, and the Server has served one fault.

RULE 12

When To Serve

The Server shall not serve until the Receiver is ready. If the latter attempts to return the service, he shall be deemed ready. If, however, the Receiver signifies that he is not ready, he may not claim a fault because the ball does not hit the ground within the limits fixed for the service.

USTA Comment: *The Server must wait until the Receiver is ready for the second service as well as the first, and if the Receiver claims to be not ready and does not make any effort to return a service, the Server's claim for the point may not be honored even though the service was good. However, the Receiver, having indicated he is ready, may not become unready unless some outside interference takes place.*

RULE 13

The Let

In all cases where a let has to be called under the rules, or to provide for an interruption to play, it shall have the following interpretations:

(a) When called solely in respect of a service that one service only shall be replayed.

(b) When called under any other circumstance, the point shall be replayed.

Case 1. A service is interrupted by some cause outside those defined in Rule 14. Should the service only be replayed?

Decision. No, the whole point must be replayed.

USTA Comment: *If a delay between first and second serves is caused by the Receiver, by an official or by an outside interference the whole point shall be replayed; if the delay is caused by the Server, the Server has one serve to come. A spectator's outcry (of "out", "fault" or other) is not a valid basis for replay of a point, but action should be taken to prevent a recurrence.*

USTA Comment: *Case 1 refers to a second serve, and the decision means that if the interruption occurs during delivery of the second service, the Server gets two serves. Example: On a second service a linesman calls "fault" and immediately corrects it, the Receiver meanwhile having let the ball go by. The Server is entitled to two serves, on this ground: The corrected call means that the Server has put the ball into play with a good service, and once the ball is in play and a let is called, the point must be replayed. Note, however, that if the serve is an unmistakable ace — that is, the Umpire is sure the erroneous call had no part in the Receiver's inability to play the ball — the point should be declared for the Server.*

Case 2. If a ball in play becomes broken, should a let be called?

Decision. Yes.

USTA Comment: *A ball shall be regarded as having become "broken" if, in the opinion of the Chair Umpire, it is found to have lost compression to the point of being unfit for further play, or unfit for any reason, and it is clear the defective ball was the one in play.*

RULE 14

The "Let" in Service

The service is a let:

(a) If the ball served touches the net, strap or band, and is otherwise good, or, after touching the net, strap or band, touches the Receiver or anything which he wears or carries before hitting the ground.

(b) If a service or a fault is delivered when the Receiver is not ready (see Rule 12).

In case of a let, that particular service shall not count, and the Server shall serve again, but a service let does not annul a previous fault.

RULE 15

Order of Service

At the end of the first game the Receiver shall become Server, and the Server Receiver; and so on alternately in all the subsequent games of a match. If a player serves out of turn, the player who ought to have served shall serve as soon as the mistake is discovered, but all points scored before such discovery shall be reckoned. If a game shall have been completed before such discovery, the order of service remains as altered. A fault served before such discovery shall not be reckoned.

RULE 16
When Players Change Ends
The players shall change ends at the end of the first, third and every subsequent alternate game of each set, and at the end of each set unless the total number of games in such set is even, in which case the change is not made until the end of the first game of the next set.

If a mistake is made and the correct sequence is not followed the players must take up their correct station as soon as the discovery is made and follow their original sequence.

RULE 17
The Ball in Play
A ball is in play from the moment at which it is delivered in service. Unless a fault or a let is called it remains in play until the point is decided.

USTA Comment: *A point is not decided simply when, or because, a good shot has clearly passed a player, or when an apparently bad shot passes over a baseline or sideline. An outgoing ball is still definitely in play until it actually strikes the ground, backstop or a permanent fixture (other than the net, posts, singles sticks, cord or metal cable, strap or band), or a player. The same applies to a good ball, bounding after it has landed in the proper court. A ball that becomes imbedded in the net is out of play.*

Case 1. A player fails to make a good return. No call is made and the ball remains in play. May his opponent later claim the point after the rally has ended?

Decision. No. The point may not be claimed if the players continue to play after the error has been made, provided the opponent was not hindered.

USTA Comment: *To be valid, an out call on A's shot to B's court, that B plays, must be made before B's shot has either gone out of play or has been hit by A. See Case 3 under Rule 29.*

USTA Comment: *When a ball is hit into the net and the player on the other side, thinking the ball is coming over, strikes at it and hits the net he loses the point if his touching the net occurs while the ball is still in play.*

RULE 18
Server Wins Point
The Server wins the point:

(a) If the ball served, not being a let under Rule 14, touches the Receiver or anything which he wears or carries, before it hits the ground;

(b) If the Receiver otherwise loses the point as provided by Rule 20.

RULE 19
Receiver Wins Point
The Receiver wins the point:

(a) If the Server serves two consecutive faults;

(b) If the Server otherwise loses the point as provided by Rule 20.

254

RULE 20

Player Loses Point

A player loses the point if:

(a) He fails, before the ball in play has hit the ground twice consecutively, to return it directly over the net (except as provided in Rule 24(a) or (c)); or

(b) He returns the ball in play so that it hits the ground, a permanent fixture, or other object, outside any of the lines which bound his opponent's Court (except as provided in Rule 24(a) or (c)); or

USTA Comment: *A ball hitting a scoring device or other object attached to a net post results in loss of point to the striker.*

(c) He volleys the ball and fails to make a good return even when standing outside the Court; or

(d) In playing the ball he deliberately carries or catches it on his racket or deliberately touches it with his racket more than once; or

USTA Comment: *Only when there is a definite "second push" by the player does his shot become illegal, with consequent loss of point. The word 'deliberately' is the key word in this rule. Two hits occurring in the course of a single continuous swing are not deemed a double hit.*

(e) He or his racket (in his hand or otherwise) or anything which he wears or carries touches the net, posts, singles sticks, cord or metal cable, strap or band, or the ground within his opponent's Court at any time while the ball is in play; or

USTA Comment: *Touching a pipe support that runs across the court at the bottom of the net is interpreted as touching the net; See USTA Comment under Rule 23.*

(f) He volleys the ball before it has passed the net; or

(g) The ball in play touches him or anything that he wears or carries, except his racket in his hand or hands; or

USTA Comment: *This loss of point occurs regardless of whether the player is inside or outside the bounds of his court when the ball touches him.*

(h) He throws his racket at and hits the ball; or

(i) He deliberately and materially changes the shape of his racket during the playing of the point.

Case 1. In serving, the racket flies from the Server's hand and touches the net before the ball has touched the ground. Is this a fault, or does the player lose the point?
Decision. The Server loses the point because his racket touches the net whilst the ball is in play (Rule 20 (e)).

Case 2. In serving, the racket flies from the Server's hand and touches the net after the ball has touched the ground outside the proper court. Is this a fault, or does the player lose the point?
Decision. This is a fault because the ball was out of play when the racket touched the net.

Case 3. A and B are playing against C and D, A is serving to D, C touches the net before the ball touches the ground. A fault is then called because the service falls outside the Service Court. Do C and D lose the point?
Decision. The call "fault" is an erroneous one. C and D had already lost the point before "fault" could be called, because C touched the net whilst the ball was in play (Rule 20 (e)).

Case 4. May a player jump over the net into his opponent's Court while the ball is in play and not suffer penalty?
Decision. No. He loses the point (Rule 20 (e)).

Case 5. A cuts the ball just over the net, and it returns to A's side. B, unable to reach the ball, throws his racket and hits the ball. Both racket and ball fall over the net on A's Court. A returns the ball outside of B's Court. Does B win or lose the point?
Decision. B loses the point (Rule 20 (e) and (h)).

Case 6. A player standing outside the service Court is struck by a service ball before it has touched the ground. Does he win or lose the point?

Decision. The player struck loses the point (Rule 20 *(g)*), except as provided under Rule 14 *(a)*.

Case 7. A player standing outside the Court volleys the ball or catches it in his hand and claims the point because the ball was certainly going out of court.

Decision. In no circumstances can he claim the point:

(1) If he catches the ball he loses the point under Rule 20 *(g)*.

(2) If he volleys it and makes a bad return he loses the point under Rule 20 *(c)*.

(3) If he volleys it and makes a good return, the rally continues.

RULE 21

Player Hinders Opponent

If a player commits any act which hinders his opponent in making a stroke, then, if this is deliberate, he shall lose the point or if involuntary, the point shall be replayed.

USTA Comment: *'Deliberate' means a player did what he intended to do, although the resulting effect on his opponent might or might not have been what he intended. Example: a player, after his return is in the air, gives advice to his partner in such a loud voice that his opponent is hindered. 'Involuntary' means a non-intentional act such as a hat blowing off or a scream resulting from a sudden wasp sting.*

Case 1. Is a player liable to a penalty if in making a stroke he touches his opponent?

Decision. No, unless the Umpire deems it necessary to take action under Rule 21.

Case 2. When a ball bounds back over the net, the player concerned may reach over the net in order to play the ball. What is the ruling if the player is hindered from doing this by his opponent?

Decision. In accordance with Rule 21, the Umpire may either award the point to the player hindered, or order the point to be replayed. (See also Rule 25).

Case 3. Does an involuntary double hit constitute an act which hinders an opponent within Rule 21?

Decision. No.

USTA Comment: *Upon appeal by a competitor that the server's action in discarding a "second ball" after a rally has started constitutes a distraction (hindrance), the Umpire, if he deems the claim valid, shall require the server to make some other and satisfactory disposition of the ball. Failure to comply with this instruction may result in loss of point(s) or disqualification.*

RULE 22

Ball Falls on Line

A ball falling on a line is regarded as falling in the Court bounded by that line.

USTA Comment: *In a non-officiated singles match, each player makes the call on any ball hit toward his side of the net, and if a player cannot call a ball out with surety he should regard it as good. See paragraph 7 of The Code and the last USTA Comment under Rule 10.*

RULE 23

Ball Touches Permanent Fixtures

If the ball in play touches a permanent fixture (other than the net, posts, singles sticks, cord or metal cable, strap or band) after it has hit the ground, the player who struck it wins the point; if before it hits the ground, his opponent wins the point.

Case 1. A return hits the Umpire or his chair or stand. The player claims that the ball was going into Court.

Decision. He loses the point.

USTA Comment: *A ball in play that after passing the net strikes a pipe support running across the court at the base of the net is regarded the same as a ball landing on clear ground. See also Rule 20(e).*

A Good Return

It is a good return:

(a) If the ball touches the net, posts, singles sticks, cord or metal cable, strap or band, provided that it passes over any of them and hits the ground within the Court; or

(b) If the ball, served or returned, hits the ground within the proper Court and rebounds or is blown back over the net, and the player whose turn it is to strike reaches over the net and plays the ball, provided that neither he nor any part of his clothes or racket touches the net, posts, singles sticks, cord or metal cable, strap or band or the ground within his opponent's Court, and that the stroke is otherwise good; or

(c) If the ball is returned outside the posts, or singles sticks, either above or below the level of the top of the net, even though it touches the posts or singles sticks, provided that it hits the ground within the proper Court; or

(d) If a player's racket passes over the net after he has returned the ball, provided the ball passes the net before being played and is properly returned; or

(e) If a player succeeds in returning the ball, served or in play, which strikes a ball lying in the Court.

USTA Comment: *Paragraph (e) of the rule refers to a ball lying on the court at the start of the point, as a result of a service let or fault, or as a result of a player dropping it. If a ball in play strikes a rolling or stationary "foreign" ball that has come from elsewhere after the point started, a let should be played. See Case 7 under Rule 25 and note that it pertains to an object other than a ball that is being used in the match.*

Note to Rule 24: In a singles match, if, for the sake of convenience, a doubles Court is equipped with singles sticks for the purpose of a singles game, then the doubles posts and those portions of the net, cord or metal cable and the band outside such singles sticks shall at all times be permanent fixtures, and are not regarded as posts or parts of the net of a singles game.

A return that passes under the net cord between the singles stick and adjacent doubles post without touching either net cord, net or doubles post and falls within the court, is a good return. **USTA Comment:** *But in doubles this would be a "through" — loss of point.*

Case 1. A ball going out of Court hits a net post or singles stick and falls within the lines of the opponent's Court. Is the stroke good?
Decision. If a service: no, under Rule 10 (c). If other than a service: yes, under Rule 24 (a).
Case 2. Is it a good return if a player returns the ball holding his racket in both hands?
Decision. Yes.
Case 3. The service, or ball in play, strikes a ball lying in the Court. Is the point won or lost thereby?
USTA Comment: *A ball that is touching a boundary line is considered to be "lying in the court".*
Decision. No. Play must continue. If it is not clear to the Umpire that the right ball is returned a let should be called.
Case 4. May a player use more than one racket at any time during play?
Decision. No; the whole implication of the Rules is singular.
Case 5. May a player request that a ball or balls lying in his opponent's Court be removed?
Decision. Yes, but not while a ball is in play. **USTA Comment:** *The request must be honored.*

RULE 25

Hindrance of a Player

In case a player is hindered in making a stroke by anything not within his control, except a permanent fixture of the Court, or except as provided for in Rule 21, a let shall be called.

Case 1. A spectator gets into the way of a player, who fails to return the ball. May the player then claim a let?

Decision. Yes, if in the Umpire's opinion he was obstructed by circumstances beyond his control, but not if due to permanent fixtures of the Court or the arrangements of the ground.

Case 2. A player is interfered with as in Case No. 1, and the Umpire calls a let. The Server had previously served a fault. Has he the right to two services?

Decision. Yes: as the ball is in play, the point, not merely the stroke, must be replayed as the Rule provides.

Case 3. May a player claim a let under Rule 25 because he thought his opponent was being hindered, and consequently did not expect the ball to be returned?

Decision. No.

Case 4. Is a stroke good when a ball in play hits another ball in the air?

Decision. A let should be called unless the other ball is in the air by the act of one of the players, in which case the Umpire will decide under Rule 21.

Case 5. If an Umpire or other judge erroneously calls "fault" or "out", and then corrects himself, which of the calls shall prevail?

Decision. A let must be called unless, in the opinion of the Umpire, neither player is hindered in his game, in which case the corrected call shall prevail.

Case 6. If the first ball served — a fault — rebounds, interfering with the Receiver at the time of the second service, may the Receiver claim a let?

Decision. Yes. But if he had an opportunity to remove the ball from the Court and negligently failed to do so, he may not claim a let.

Case 7. Is it a good stroke if the ball touches a stationary or moving object on the Court?

Decision. It is a good stroke unless the stationary object came into Court after the ball was put into play in which case a let must be called. If the ball in play strikes an object moving along or above the surface of the Court a let must be called.

Case 8. What is the ruling if the first service is a fault, the second service correct, and it becomes necessary to call a let either under the provision of Rule 25 or if the Umpire is unable to decide the point?

Decision. The fault shall be annulled and the whole point replayed.

USTA Comment: *See Rule 13 with its USTA Comments.*

RULE 26

Score in a Game

If a player wins his first point, the score is called 15 for that player; on winning his second point, the score is called 30 for that player; on winning his third point, the score is called 40 for that player, and the fourth point won by a player is scored game for that player except as below:

If both players have won three points, the score is called deuce; and the next point won by a player is scored advantage for that player. If the same player wins the next point, he wins the game; if the other player wins the next point the score is again called deuce; and so on, until a player wins the two points immediately following the score at deuce, when the game is scored for that player.

USTA Comment: *In a non-officiated match the Server should announce, in a voice audible to his opponent and spectators, the set score at the beginning of each game, and point scores as the game goes on. Misunderstandings will be avoided if this practice is followed.*

Score in a Set

(a) A player (or players) who first wins six games wins a set; except that he must win by a margin of two games over his opponent and where necessary a set is extended until this margin is achieved.

(b) The tie-break system of scoring may be adopted as an alternative to the advantage set system in paragraph (a) of this Rule provided the decision is announced in advance of the match.

USTA Comment: *See the Tie-Break System near the middle of this book.*

In this case, the following Rules shall be effective:

The tie-break shall operate when the score reaches six games all in any set except in the third or fifth set of a three set or five set match respectively when an ordinary advantage set shall be played, unless otherwise decided and announced in advance of the match.

The following system shall be used in a tie-break game.

Singles

(i) A player who first wins seven points shall win the game and the set provided he leads by a margin of two points. If the score reaches six points all the game shall be extended until this margin has been achieved. Numerical scoring shall be used throughout the tie-break game.

(ii) The player whose turn it is to serve shall be the server for the first point. His opponent shall be the server for the second and third points and thereafter each player shall serve alternately for two consecutive points until the winner of the game and set has been decided.

(iii) From the first point, each service shall be delivered alternately from the right and left courts, beginning from the right court. If service from a wrong half of the court occurs and is undetected, all play resulting from such wrong service or services shall stand, but the inaccuracy of station shall be corrected immediately it is discovered.

(iv) Players shall change ends after every six points and at the conclusion of the tie-break game.

(v) The tie-break game shall count as one game for the ball change, except that, if the balls are due to be changed at the beginning of the tie-break, the change shall be delayed until the second game of the following set.

Doubles

In doubles the procedure for singles shall apply. The player whose turn it is to serve shall be the server for the first point. Thereafter each player shall serve in rotation for two points, in the same order as previously in that set, until the winners of the game and set have been decided.

Rotation of Service

The player (or pair in the case of doubles) who served first in the tie-break game shall receive service in the first game of the following set.

Case 1. At six all the tie-break is played, although it has been decided and announced in advance of the match that an advantage set will be played. Are the points already played counted?

Decision. If the error is discovered before the ball is put in play for the second point, the first point shall count but the error shall be corrected immediately. If the error is discovered after the ball is put in play for the second point the game shall continue as a tie-break game.

Case 2. At six all, an advantage game is played, although it has been decided and announced in advance of the match that a tie-break will be played. Are the points already played counted?

Decision. If the error is discovered before the ball is put in play for the second point, the first point shall be counted but the error shall be corrected immediately. If the error is discovered after the ball is put in play for the second point an advantage set shall be continued. If the score thereafter reaches eight games all or a higher even number, a tie-break shall be played.

Case 3. If during a tie-break in a singles or doubles game, a player serves out of turn, shall the order of service remain as altered until the end of the game?

Decision. If a player has completed his turn of service the order of service shall remain as altered. If the error is discovered before a player has completed his turn of service the order of service shall be corrected immediately and any points already played shall count.

RULE 28
Maximum Number of Sets

The maximum number of sets in a match shall be 5, or, where women take part, 3.

RULE 29
Role of Court Officials

In matches where an Umpire is appointed, his decision shall be final; but where a Referee is appointed, an appeal shall lie to him from the decision of an Umpire on a question of law, and in all such cases the decision of the Referee shall be final.

In matches where assistants to the Umpire are appointed (Linesmen, Net-cord Judges, Foot-fault Judges) their decisions shall be final on questions of fact except that if in the opinion of an Umpire a clear mistake has been made he shall have the right to change the decision of an assistant or order a let to be played. When such an assistant is unable to give a decision he shall indicate this immediately to the Umpire who shall give a decision. When an Umpire is unable to give a decision on a question of fact he shall order a let to be played.

In Davis Cup matches or other team competitions where a Referee is on Court, any decision can be changed by the Referee, who may also instruct an Umpire to order a let to be played.

The Referee, in his discretion, may at any time postpone a match on account of darkness or the condition of the ground or the weather. In any case of postponement the previous score and previous occupancy of Courts shall hold good, unless the Referee and the players unanimously agree otherwise.

USTA Comment: *See second USTA Comment under Rule 30.*

Case 1. The Umpire orders a let, but a player claims that the point should not be replayed. May the Referee be requested to give a decision?

Decision. Yes. A question of tennis law, that is an issue relating to the application of specific facts, shall first be determined by the Umpire. However, if the Umpire is uncertain or if a player appeals from his determination, then the Referee shall be requested to give a decision, and his decision is final.

Case 2. A ball is called out, but a player claims that the ball was good. May the Referee give a ruling?

Decision. No. This is a question of fact, that is an issue relating to what actually occurred during a specific incident, and the decision of the on-court officials is therefore final.

Case 3. May an Umpire overrule a Linesman at the end of a rally if, in his opinion, a clear mistake has been made during the course of a rally?

Decision. No, unless in his opinion the opponent was hindered. Otherwise an Umpire may only overrule a Linesman if he does so immediately after the mistake has been made.

USTA Comment: *See Rule 17, Case 1.*

Case 4. A Linesman calls a ball out. The Umpire was unable to see clearly, although he thought the ball was in. May he overrule the Linesman?

Decision. No. An Umpire may only overrule if he considers that a call was incorrect beyond all reasonable doubt. He may only overrule a ball determined good by a Linesman if he has been able to see a space between the ball and the line; and he may only overrule a ball determined out, or a fault, by a Linesman if he has seen the ball hit the line, or fall inside the line.

Case 5. May a Linesman change his call after the Umpire has given the score?

Decision. Yes. If a Linesman realises he has made an error, he may make a correction provided he does so immediately.

Case 6. A player claims his return shot was good after a Linesman called "out". May the Umpire overrule the Linesman?

Decision. No. An Umpire may never overrule as a result of a protest or an appeal by a player.

RULE 30

Continuous Play and Rest Periods

Play shall be continuous from the first service until the match is concluded, in accordance with the following provisions:

(a) If the first service is a fault, the second service must be struck by the Server without delay.

The Receiver must play to the reasonable pace of the Server and must be ready to receive when the Server is ready to serve.

When changing ends a maximum of one minute thirty seconds shall elapse from the moment the ball goes out of play at the end of the game to the time the ball is struck for the first point of the next game.

The Umpire shall use his discretion when there is interference which makes it impractical for play to be continuous.

The organizers of international circuits and team events recognized by the ITF may determine the time allowed between points, which shall not at any time exceed 30 seconds.

(b) Play shall never be suspended, delayed or interfered with for the purpose of enabling a player to recover his strength, breath, or physical condition.

However, in the case of accidental injury, the Umpire may allow a one-time three minute suspension for that injury.

The organizers of international circuits and team events recognized by the ITF may extend the one-time suspension period from three minutes to five minutes.

USTA Comment: *All players must follow the same rules with respect to suspending play, even though in misty, but playable, weather a player who wears glasses may be handicapped.*

(c) If, through circumstances outside the control of the player, his clothing, footwear or equipment (excluding racket) becomes out of adjustment in such a way that it is impossible or undesirable for him to play on, the Umpire may suspend play while the maladjustment is rectified.

USTA Comment: *Loss of, or damage to, a contact lens or eyeglasses shall be treated as equipment maladjustment.*

(d) The Umpire may suspend or delay play at any time as may be necessary and appropriate.

USTA Comment: *When a match is resumed after a suspension of more than ten minutes, it is permissible for the players to engage in a re-warm-up that may be of the same duration as that at the start of the match. The preferred method is to warm-up with other used balls and then insert the match balls when play starts. If the match balls are used in the re-warm-up, then the next ball change will be two games sooner. There shall be no re-warm-up after an authorized intermission or after a suspension of ten minutes or less.*

(e) After the third set, or when women take part the second set, either player is entitled to a rest, which shall not exceed 10 minutes, or in countries situated between latitude 15 degrees north and latitude 15 degrees south, 45 minutes and furthermore, when necessitated by circumstances not within the control of the players, the Umpire may suspend play for such a period as he may consider necessary. If play is suspended and is not resumed until a later day the rest may be taken only after the third set (or when women take part the second set) of play on such a later day, completion of an unfinished set being counted as one set.

If play is suspended and is not resumed until 10 minutes have elapsed in the same day the rest may be taken only after three consecutive sets have been played without interruption (or when women take part two sets), completion of an unfinished set being counted as one set.

Any nation and/or committee organizing a tournament, match or competition, other than the International Tennis Championships (Davis Cup and Federation Cup), is at liberty to modify this provision or omit it from its regulations provided this is announced before the event commences.

(f) A tournament committee has the discretion to decide the time allowed for a warm-up period prior to a match but this may not exceed five minutes and must be announced before the event commences.

USTA Comment: *When there are no ballpersons this time may be extended to ten minutes.*

(g) When approved point penalty and non-accumulative point penalty systems are in operation, the Umpire shall make his decisions within the terms of those systems.

(h) Upon violation of the principle that play shall be continuous the Umpire may, after giving due warning, disqualify the offender.

RULE 31
Coaching

During the playing of a match in a team competition, a player may receive coaching from a captain who is sitting on the court only when he changes ends at the end of a game, but not when he changes ends during a tie-break game.

A player may not receive coaching during the playing of any other match.

After due warning an offending player may be disqualified. When an approved point penalty system is in operation, the Umpire shall impose penalties according to that system.

Case 1. Should a warning be given, or the player be disqualified, if the coaching is given by signals in an unobtrusive manner?

Decision. The Umpire must take action as soon as he becomes aware that coaching is being given verbally or by signals. If the Umpire is unaware that coaching is being given, a player may draw his attention to the fact that advice is being given.

Case 2. Can a player receive coaching during an authorized rest period under Rule 30(e), or when play is interrupted and he leaves the court?

Decision. Yes. In these circumstances, when the player is not on the court, there is no restriction on coaching.

Note: The word "coaching" includes any advice or instruction.

RULE 32
Changing Balls

In cases where balls are to be changed after a specified number of games, if the balls are not changed in the correct sequence, the mistake shall be corrected when the player, or pair in the case of doubles, who should have served with new balls is next due to serve. Thereafter the balls shall be changed so that the number of games between changes shall be that originally agreed.

The Doubles Game

RULE 33

The above Rules shall apply to the Doubles Game except as below.

RULE 34

The Doubles Court

For the Doubles Game, the Court shall be 36 feet (10.97m.) in width, i.e. 4½ feet (1.37m.) wider on each side than the Court for the Singles Game, and those portions of the singles side-lines which lie between the two service-lines shall be called the service side-lines. In other respects, the Court shall be similar to that described in Rule 1, but the portions of the singles side-lines between the base-line and service-line on each side of the net may be omitted if desired.

USTA Comment: *The Server has the right in doubles to stand anywhere back of the baseline between the center mark imaginary extension and the doubles sideline imaginary extension.*

RULE 35

Order of Service in Doubles

The order of serving shall be decided at the beginning of each set as follows:

The pair who have to serve in the first game of each set shall decide which partner shall do so and the opposing pair shall decide similarly for the second game. The partner of the player who served in the first game shall serve in the third; the partner of the player who served in the second game shall serve in the fourth, and so on in the same order in all the subsequent games of a set.

Case 1. In doubles, one player does not appear in time to play, and his partner claims to be allowed to play single-handed against the opposing players. May he do so?
Decision. No.

RULE 36

Order of Receiving in Doubles

The order of receiving the service shall be decided at the beginning of each set as follows:

The pair who have to receive the service in the first game shall decide which partner shall receive the first service, and that partner shall continue to receive the first service in every odd game throughout that set. The opposing pair shall likewise decide which partner shall receive the first service in the second game and that partner shall continue to receive the first service in every even game throughout that set. Partners shall receive the service alternately throughout each game.

Case 1. Is it allowable in doubles for the Server's partner or the Receiver's partner to stand in a position that obstructs the view of the Receiver?
Decision. Yes. The Server's partner or the Receiver's partner may take any position on his side of the net in or out of the Court that he wishes.

RULE 37

Service Out of Turn in Doubles

If a partner serves out of his turn, the partner who ought to have served shall serve as soon as the mistake is discovered, but all points scored, and any faults served before such discovery, shall be reckoned. If a game shall have been completed before such discovery, the order of service remains as altered.

USTA Comment: *For an exception to Rule 37 see Case 3 under Rule 27.*

RULE 38

Error in Order of Receiving in Doubles

If during a game the order of receiving the service is changed by the Receivers it shall remain as altered until the end of the game in which the mistake is discovered, but the partners shall resume their original order of receiving in the next game of that set in which they are Receivers of the service.

RULE 39

Service Fault in Doubles

The service is a fault as provided for by Rule 10, or if the ball touches the Server's partner or anything which he wears or carries; but if the ball served touches the partner of the Receiver, or anything which he wears or carries, not being a let under Rule 14(a) before it hits the ground, the Server wins the point.

RULE 40

Playing the Ball in Doubles

The ball shall be struck alternately by one or other player of the opposing pairs, and if a player touches the ball in play with his racket in contravention of this Rule, his opponents win the point.

USTA Comment: *This means that, in the course of making one return, only one member of a doubles team may hit the ball. If both of them hit the ball, either simultaneously or consecutively, it is an illegal return. The partners themselves do not have to "alternate" in making returns. Mere clashing of rackets does not make a return illegal unless it is clear that more than one racket touched the ball.*

APPENDIX I
Regulations for Making Tests Specified in Rule 3

1. Unless otherwise specified all tests shall be made at a temperature of approximately 68° Fahrenheit (20° Centigrade) and a relative humidity of approximately 60 per cent. All balls should be removed from their container and kept at the recognized temperature and humidity for 24 hours prior to testing, and shall be at that temperature and humidity when the test is commenced.

2. Unless otherwise specified the limits are for a test conducted in an atmospheric pressure resulting in a barometric reading of approximately 30 inches (76cm.).

3. Other standards may be fixed for localities where the average temperature, humidity or average barometric pressure at which the game is being played differ materially from 68° Fahrenheit (20° Centigrade), 60 per cent and 30 inches (76cm.) respectively.

Applications for such adjusted standards may be made by any National Association to the International Tennis Federation and if approved shall be adopted for such localities.

4. In all tests for diameter a ring gauge shall be used consisting of a metal plate, preferably non-corrosive, of a uniform thickness of one-eighth of an inch (.32cm.) in which there are two circular openings 2.575 inches (6.54cm.) and 2.700 inches (6.86cm.) in diameter respectively. The inner surface of the gauge shall have a convex profile with a radius of one-sixteenth of an inch. (.16cm.). The ball shall not drop through the smaller opening by its own weight and shall drop through the larger opening by its own weight.

5. In all tests for deformation conducted under Rule 3, the machine designed by Percy Herbert Stevens and patented in Great Britain under Patent No. 230250, together with the subsequent additions and improvements thereto, including the modifications required to take return deformations, shall be employed or such other machine which is approved by a National Association and gives equivalent readings to the Stevens machine.

6. Procedure for carrying out tests.

(a) Pre-compression. Before any ball is tested it shall be steadily compressed by approximately one inch (2.54cm.) on each of three diameters at right angles to one another in succession; this process to be carried out three times (nine compressions in all). All tests to be completed within two hours of precompression.

(b) Bound test (as in Rule 3). Measurements are to be taken from the concrete base to the bottom of the ball.

(c) Size test (as in paragraph 4 above).

(d) Weight test (as in Rule 3).

(e) Deformation test. The ball is placed in position on the modified Stevens machine so that neither platen of the machine is in contact with the cover seam. The contact weight is applied, the pointer and the mark brought level, and the dials set to zero. The test weight equivalent to 18 lb. (8.165kg.) is placed on the beam and pressure applied by turning the wheel at a uniform speed so that five seconds elapse from the instant the beam leaves its seat until the pointer is brought level with the mark. When turning ceases the reading is recorded (forward deformation). The wheel is turned again until figure ten is reached on the scale (one inch [2.54 cm.] deformation). The wheel is then rotated in the opposite direction at a uniform speed (thus releasing pressure) until the beam pointer again coincides with the mark. After waiting ten seconds the pointer is adjusted to the mark if necessary. The reading is then recorded (return deformation). This procedure is repeated on each ball across the two diameters at right angles to the initial position and to each other.

APPENDIX II
Rules of Wheelchair Tennis

The Rules of Tennis shall apply to wheelchair tennis with the following exceptions:

1. The wheelchair player is allowed two bounces.
2. The first bounce must land inside the court boundaries.
3. Service must be initiated with both rear wheels behind the baseline.
4. The Chair is part of the body. All applicable rules apply.

(a) A player loses the point if the ball in play touches him or his wheelchair or anything he wears or carries, except his racket in his hand(s). This loss of a point occurs regardless of whether the player is inside or outside the bounds of his court when the ball touches him.

(b) The player loses the point if a served ball hits him or his wheelchair or anything he carries, except his racket in his hand(s). If the server hits his own partner with the served ball, then it is a fault.

(c) A wheel fault is incurred if during the delivery of the service either of the rear wheels touches any area other than that behind the baseline within the imaginary extensions of the center mark and side lines. The front wheels may be situated over the baseline and/or center lines.

The Tie-Breaks and VASSS Scoring

1) *Use must be announced before tournament starts.* The tournament committee must announce before the start of its tournament the details concerning its use of tie-breaks.

2) *Twelve-point tie-break must normally be used.* If a sanctioned tournament uses tie-breaks it must use the 12-point tie-break unless it is authorized to use the nine-point tie-break pursuant to Tournament Regulation P3.

3) *When VASSS, No-Ad and Nine-Point tie-breaks are authorized.* No-Ad scoring is authorized for tournaments held at the sectional championship level and below, and for consolation matches in any tournament (excluding any USTA National Junior Championship). A tournament that has been authorized by the USTA or by a USTA section to use VASSS No-Ad scoring may use the nine-point tie-break in any set played under No-Ad. It may change to the 12-point tie-break in its later rounds.

4) *Ball changes.* If a ball change is due on a tie-break game it will be deferred until the second game of the next set. A tie-break game counts as one game in reckoning ball changes.

5) *Recording the tie-break score.* The score of the tie-break set will be written 7-6 (x) or 6-7 (x), with (x) being the number of points won by the loser of the tie-break. For example, 7-6 (4) means the tie-break score was 7-4, and 6-7 (14) means the tie-break score was 14-16.

6) *Changing ends during the tie-break.* Changes of ends during a tie-break game are to be made within the normal time allowed between points.

7) *Twelve-point tie-break.*

   Singles: A, having served first game of the set, serves the first point from the right court; B serves points 2 and 3 (left and right); A serves points 4 and 5 (left and right); B serves point 6 (left) and after they change ends, point 7 (right); A serves points 8 and 9 (left and right); B serves points 10 and 11 (left and right); A serves point 12 (left). A player who reaches seven points during these first 12 points wins the game and set. If the score has reached six points all, the players change ends and continue in the same pattern until one player establishes a margin of two points which gives him the game and set. Note that the players change ends every six points and that the player who serves the last point of one of these 6-point segments also serves the first point of the next one (from right court). For a following set the players change ends and B serves the first game.

   Doubles: The same pattern as in singles applies, with partners preserving their serving sequence. In a game of A-B versus C-D, with A having served the first game of the set, A serves the first point (right); C serves points 2 and 3 (left and right); B serves points 4 and 5 (left and right); D serves point 6 (left) and after the teams change ends, D serves point 7 (right); A serves points 8 and 9 (left and right); C serves points 10 and 11 (left and right); B serves point 12 (left). A team that wins seven points during these first 12 points wins the game and set. If the score has reached six points all, the teams change ends. B then serves point 13 (right), and they continue until one team establishes a two-point margin and thus wins the game and set. As in singles, they change ends for one game to start a following set, with team C-D to serve first.

8) *Nine-point tie-break.*

Singles: A, having served the first game of the set, serves points 1 and 2, right court and left; B serves points 3 and 4 (right and left) players change ends; A serves points 5 and 6 (right and left); B serves points 7 and 8 (right and left). If the score reaches 4 points all, B serves point 9, right or left at the election of A. The first player to win 5 points wins the game and set. The players stay for one game to start the next set and B is the first server.

Doubles: The same format as in singles applies, with each player serving from the same end of the court in the tie-break game that he served from during the set. (Note that this operates to alter the sequence of serving by the partners on the second-serving team. With A-B versus C-D, if the serving sequence during the set was A-C-B-D the sequence becomes A-D-B-C in the tie-break.).

9) *No-Ad scoring.* The No-Ad procedure is simply what the name implies: the first player to win four points wins the game, with the seventh point of a game becoming a game point for each player. The receiver has the choice of advantage court or deuce court to which the service is to be delivered on the seventh point. If a No-Ad set reaches six-games all a tie-break shall be used, which is normally the nine-point tie-break.

Note: The score-calling may be either in the conventional terms or in simple numbers, i.e., "zero, one, two, three, game."

Cautionary Note: Any ITF-sponsored tournament should get special authorization from ITF before using No-Ad.

10) *Experimental tie-break procedure.* For experimental purposes, a section may authorize any tournament below the national championship level to use an amended 12-point tie-break that is the same as the present 12-point tie-break except that ends are changed after the first point, then after every four points, and at the conclusion of the tie-break game. This authorization is with the provisos that all 12-point tie-breaks in the tournament be so played, that any tournament utilizing this amended tie-break announce it in advance of the tournament and that each tournament so involved send a detailed report concerning the merits of the experiment to the Sectional President, with a copy to the Chairman, USTA Tennis Rules Committee.

268

INDEX OF THE RULES OF TENNIS

272

INDEX